Dearest Kevin ♡ Joe,

We would love to be able to connect with you again. May God continue to bless your journey.

Love,

Ed ♡ Betty

Reality TV shows like Jon & Kate plus 8, Table for 12, & 17 and counting, all show us how hard life and marriage are when trying to raise strong, intelligent, kind-hearted children. All parents, no matter the size of their family, need to see and believe that it is possible to live their lives, nurturingly raise their children, and still maintain and even improve their love and passion for each other. Ed & Betty are living proof.

—Chryslyn Hayes, Daughter of Ed & Betty

Ed and Betty Coda's love and passion for each other and their close family relationships are very visible and contagious. We have known Ed and Betty for over 30 years and whenever we are with them, they touch our hearts with their warmth, joy and deep commitment to continually work on having an exciting and passionate marriage relationship and maintaining a close family bond with all of their children.

—Eunice Paglinawan

"When I'm with Ed and Betty, there's a feeling of peace and acceptance for who I am. I know that they are listening when I express my thoughts or feelings.....They are compassionate and will go the distance for you".

—Vic Canubida

They are the real deal! The Coda family lives what they preach. We've seen many of the concepts outlined in the book in practice in their family. As parents of a family with two young kids, we feel fortunate to know Ed and Betty and benefit from their advice, encouragement, and their example.

—Teresa Hei

I have observed first-hand the unbridled success these concepts have produced in every family that applies them. Ed and Betty Coda have perfected the "recipes", now it's time for us to "cook" successful families with those recipes. I have closely observed Ed, Betty and their family for over 20 years....

this stuff works.

—Janice Takemoto-Gentile

The Codas' writing of a book on parenting could not be more appropriate. To witness their family in action is the epitome of how a family should be. Their love for each other is truly visible in their children and grandchildren.

—Ron Gochenouer

Ed and Betty are an inspiration to us as a couple and as parents as we observe them in their own relationship and in their relationships with their children.

—Lauren and Hazel Wong

As a newly married couple, having a model of what lasting love looks like - while balancing both family & career - is essential to us. Ed & Betty Coda have long been our model of what real, lasting love looks like in action. We have had the honor to witness the results they have produced in their own lives and hope to create such love in our own relationship. They are the best example we know of what living in love is all about.

—Gabe and Iris Stepanic

I have known Ed and Betty for many years. I not only have experienced Ed and Betty as a couple in marriage and friends with joy, but I have also had the pleasure of knowing Ed and Betty as passionate and loving parents to me as if I were their own. My husband and I have witnessed their success in all aspects of life. We only hope to follow the same path and be as honestly happy as they are.

—Brianna & Julio Fuentes

Betty and Ed are our dear friends that always gave us good advice, so we made them our parenting consultants. It is their counsel on making our marriage the center of our lives that provides our kids with the security to be themselves. We are so grateful to have them in our lives!

—Jay Trygstad

In Ed and Betty's sharing of their relationship with us, we have seen the struggles that couples go through. They bare themselves to us, giving me hope and renewing my belief in a passionate, accepting, and forgiving marriage. They are an inspiration to me.

—Teresa Gochenouer

"The Word was made flesh and dwelt among us." These words from the first chapter of the Gospel of John summarize the most wonderful thing God has done for us. He became one of us in Jesus Christ, forever uniting human flesh and divine life. This volume by Ed and Betty Coda makes more explicit that union between divine and human, flesh and spirit that is God's plan for us all, especially for married couples. It is a gift to remind us that God wants to meet us in the ordinary aspects of our lives.

—Most Reverend Larry Silva, Catholic Bishop of Honolulu

Ed and Betty Coda are inspirational. They played a large role in the reason our family exists today. From their knowledge of Natural Family Planning to their inherent love and passion for people, parenthood, and progeny, Ed and Betty are the ultimate example of family excellence.

—Aaron & Kimberly Meyer

Passionate Parent
Passionate Couple

Keeping the passion alive
after the children arrive

Passionate Parent Passionate Couple

Keeping the passion alive
after the children arrive

ED & BETTY CODA

TAG Publishing, LLC
2618 S. Lipscomb
Amarillo, TX 79109
www.TAGPublishers.com

Office (806) 373-0114
Fax (806) 373-4004
info@TAGPublishers.com

ISBN: 978-1-59930-351-2

Cover: Daniela Savone
Text: Lloyd Arbour, www.tablloyd.com

First Edition

Dedications

To our beautiful children who have been our
greatest source of inspiration.

Foreword

I first met Ed and Betty at Our Lady of Sorrows School and Ho`ala School where I taught and our children grew to be friends. We learned from Sr. Joan Madden, founder of the Ho`ala Educational Philosophy, that "You teach who you are". In *Passionate Parent Passionate Couple*, Ed and Betty share this philosophy with their readers. As an administrator of a charter middle school in Napa, California, I have taken this lesson to heart as well. I train my faculty to consciously reflect on themselves and the implicit lessons they've learned through the process of self discovery. Our students don't just learn through teaching they learn through example. The modeling we do as teachers is hugely impactful in the lives of our students.

Even more profound however is the modeling done by parents. Ed and Betty put it so eloquently in their book: *Most parenting skills are based on working on yourself and becoming who you want to be and who you want your children to see.* True, we give birth and life to our children, yet they give back to us in the many opportunities to parent. We make mistakes and learn from them as well as become aware of our unconscious habits and turn them into gems of insight about ourselves. The more intentional we are in our parenting about what we want our children to be, the more parenting becomes an opportunity for our own personal growth and development into whole and healthy human beings. In so doing, we help nurture whole and healthy children.

Passionate Parent Passionate Couple is meditation of this process. It is meant to be read with many pauses to savor and reflect. Mahalo, Ed and Betty, for your commitment to your own personal growth, flourishing relationship, children, and sharing your wisdom with us in *Passionate Parent Passionate Couple*. You teach who you are.

—Linda Inlay, Principal

RIVER
SCHOOL

www.riverschool.org

Acknowledgements

As we began to list the people who have been so instrumental in our journey we realized that this acknowledgement would be longer than our book. We have been so blessed by our involvement with so many. So we just want to dedicate this to our parents and siblings who participated in our formation and gave us our values, foundation, and zest for life. Our children, who played our silly games, participated in what they sometimes called Forced Family Fun and taught us to be parents. Worldwide Marriage Encounter founded by Fr. Chuck Gallagher, where we learned to be a couple and make the couple the heart of the family. Ho'ala School founded by Sr. Joan Madden, where we truly honed our parenting skills and where we were challenged to take personal responsibility for the results we were getting in our parenting. The Couple to Couple League for Natural Family Planning which challenged us most in our spiritual development and faith in our God. And lastly the experiences and involvements that have kept us on our path as a passionate couple including Living in Love, Christopher West's Theology of the Body Institute, PSI, Catholic Engaged Encounter, Sarano Kelley Inc., Smart Marriages and so many more.

Of course every organization is an empty shell without its people and that is where our acknowledgements encompass the hundreds of people that have rubbed shoulders with us and whose dedication to relationship has rubbed off on us and made them our mentors, counselors, friends, confidants, teachers, coaches, and inspiration along the way.

Contents

Introduction

We were children of the sixties. Baby Boomers. Hippies. Growing up in a time of questioning and the exploration of new ideas. There were so many things that we didn't know, and we learned many of them the hard way. Living with the memory of what we did made it difficult at times to be as firm and clear as we needed to be about what we expected of our children. We give you the story of our lives to help you know what we've learned.

We met and fell in love in our first year of college and decided to wait until we finished school before we married. The song that kept us going was "Wouldn't It Be Nice?" by the Beach Boys. We believed that "No Two People Had Ever Been So in Love," as Danny Kay and Jane Wyman sang it and that, no matter what life threw at us, we could handle it.

We had four years of wedded bliss before the first of six children arrived, and we vowed to hang on to the bliss in the midst of busy lives. Jennifer (Jenny) is our first-born, who fulfilled our dream of being parents; she is the typical responsible, down-to-earth, super-logical child. This is very common to children of her birth order in the family. Anthony (Tony) is our first son, who fulfilled our dream of having boys; he is the fun-loving, witty sports enthusiast who keeps us from getting too serious. Kelleen (Kellie) with the challenges she presented for us is the one who most gave us the gift of learning to be great parents, and she takes care of our family and others with her gift of healing. Daniel (Danny) is the thinker who, because he was a breeze to raise, we often took for granted, assuming that he would make good choices without our parental input. Now he keeps us reflective and on our toes about what's next in our lives. Chryslyn

(Chrysy) is the cutest little lover, always making everyone feel good about themselves with a knack for getting huge tasks done while making them look easy. Molly is the genuine peacemaker who helps others realize their strengths and learn how to work together harmoniously.

Little by little, we learned that we could not handle our lives even with college degrees! We discovered that we could not do it alone, although we had previously thought we could. We received our best training and support from marriage enrichments like Worldwide Marriage Encounter™ and Living in Love™, parenting courses from Ho'ala School, and nurturing classes, as well as from our best friends and children. In our desire to communicate to others what we have been learning and successfully living, we've spent over 30 years as presenters for various couple and family experiences as well as certified instructors for the Couple to Couple League for Natural Family Planning™ . And now we share our knowledge with you...

Chapter 1
Passionate Parents Are a Passionate Couple

In Hollywood, a marriage is a success if it outlasts milk.

—**Rita Rudner**

Soccer practice! Dirty diapers! Ballet! Homework! Help! Today, more than ever, our families are on the move from one activity to another. That's great, right? Idle hands are the devil's playground after all. But while you and your spouse are running around town like the Tasmanian Devil, what's happening to your relationship? Once upon a time, you raced home just to see each other; you couldn't get enough. Now you pray for a traffic jam just so that you can have a few minutes to yourself before you have to explain the Pythagorean Theorem.

Children are one of God's greatest gifts, but they can take a toll on the emotional and physical intimacy in your marriage. Those of you who have children know that you walk out of the delivery room into a time warp. Before you realize it, your little bundle of joy has graduated from high school, and you and your spouse are left in an empty house staring at each other like strangers. Kids are demanding, and their needs are often immediate. If the two of you are cuddling in front of a cozy fire and little Johnny vomits his nachos or little Suzie screams bloody murder because she thinks there's a monster in her closet, you can't ignore them. Our idea of togetherness is definitely not scrubbing vomit out of the carpet. Trust us; nothing ruins the moment more than the smell of barf wafting up as you go to kiss each other. We foolishly thought that once our kids got older, we would have more time together. Quickly, we learned that time was even more precious. Between running kids to school, church, and practice and taking care of our own work and activities, we hardly ever saw each other. Finding time for sex seemed impossible.

It's easy for parents to forget to cultivate passion and closeness within their marriage with all of the demands put upon them. Whether you stay at home with your children or work outside the home, your days consist of meeting constant expectations. Being a parent is both physically and mentally exhausting, so it makes perfect sense that many couples can barely crawl into bed at night, much less think about lovemaking. So, how do you keep from losing your identity to your children; how do you be a good parent while keeping the passion alive in your marriage? Sound impossible? They once thought that putting a man on the moon wasn't feasible either. This is a critical question to be answered because as soon as a couple has children, everything changes forever. It is difficult to give each other 100 percent of your attention, to pick up and leave at the drop of a hat, or even to do many of the everyday activities that you did before the baby. For us, our days of going golfing or to a movie without any care or worry were over. With the arrival of a little one, everything revolved around a new life, and we felt a huge responsibility.

No, No Honey, You Have to Sleep in Your Own Bed Tonight

For your marriage to be successful, you absolutely have to put your relationship with your spouse first and your kids second. Now, we know that some of you reading this may think that's an incredibly selfish statement. As the airplane analogy goes, put your oxygen mask on first so you can function enough to help someone else. But even before you can be a beneficial part of any relationship, you have to first be able to have a healthy relationship with yourself. In order to do this, however, you have to know what you want. You can't give yourself freely to your husband or wife if you don't know who you are and what you want out of this life. Alone time gives you the means to ponder the yearnings of your desires.

As parents, the majority of our lives is spent in the company of others, and we are often drawn away from our own needs. Sometimes you just have to say, "Find the remote control yourself; I need some me time." Learning to turn your thoughts inward and discovering ways to listen to your own voice can bring you back to yourself in a profound and meaningful way. The more you become attuned to yourself, the better parent and spouse you will be. Meditating and dialoguing are fabulous ways to connect with yourself. We only need to find 20 minutes for meditation and 20 minutes for dialogue out of a 24-hour day to make such a profound difference.

Meditation helps us to get in touch with each other on a much higher plane. You may be thinking to yourself, "Meditation: what does that have to do with being a passionate couple?" For us, meditation makes us grounded, focused, and centered. When we take the time to clear our minds, we don't make offhanded comments. We stop living in reaction to our feelings. There is no need to say nasty remarks or get revenge when we feel hurt. Instead, we're free to be the person that we want to be, not someone that we're expected to be. It is freeing and empowering to choose who you want to be instead of being buffeted by the wind. Meditation allows us to start over and to feel connected, aligned, grounded, guided, and guarded by God.

"Meditation helps to relieve stress in me. It calms and restores my soul. While my usual prayer is talking to, asking, or praising God, meditation helps me to envision and to listen to God. All of these things make me more loving and keep my curt personality at bay. I put Ed first, after God, of course. It helps me to be more spiritual. Everything is possible with God, and I think more about God. He's more present in my life. I experienced a silent retreat in which I learned about God speaking to me, and this is lived out through daily meditation as I take this time to listen to Him. All of this makes me feel confident and secure. If God is with us, who can be against us?" —Betty

The process of dialoguing is first, writing about certain aspects of our relationship and second, sharing what we have written with each other. We can choose a question for problem solving or simply a topic that we want to talk about. The most important part, however, is making sure that it includes how each of us feels. When you write, you can be yourself and truly dive into your most intimate feelings without the fear of being judged, because feelings are neither right nor wrong. They have no morality; they just spontaneously happen.

This means that you are free to put on paper your true emotions and make great discoveries about yourself, as it frequently takes off the first layer of the onion and lets you find out what is really going on beneath the surface. Dialoguing is this freeing way of regurgitating the real you on paper and giving it to your spouse as a gift during the sharing time. It helps you to sort out your ups and downs inside to get to the bottom line. So what is the bottom line? What is the core? You simply can't have passion without knowledge of yourself.

Dialoguing gives you insight into yourself so that you can be more giving to your spouse. It provides the atmosphere where real listening can happen at the deepest levels as you read what you have written to each other. When you listen to hear who the other person is through their feelings, and at times actually experience what they are experiencing, you give each other a tremendous gift.

"Writing without seeing Betty's expressions or reactions allows me to be totally honest and get what is really going on inside me down on paper. When I share with Betty after writing, I know that she's getting the real me and not the me that I'm afraid she wanted or the me that I feel like I need to be for her, but the real me. This process has helped me to feel free and connected, and when I do share openly in this style, I know that Betty really loves me for my sake, not just because of what I do to please her. For me it's a very powerful tool that seems to be the best way to get a real, honest communication and deep sharing going with Betty." —Ed

As you begin to discover insights into your life, you might consider asking questions like "What is most important to me?" or "How can I be a better partner?" or "What is it about me that adds or detracts from our relationship?" After writing an answer to these questions, you might notice that it is easier to listen to the things that you need to consider and hear. Discoveries that you make will also make you feel good about yourself. The better you feel about yourself, the greater the chances for enhancing your relationships with others. We know it is not easy to find even the few minutes needed for these practices, and yes, there are some times when we just nod off in pure exhaustion, but the times when we are successful are truly worthwhile.

The Couple Is the Heart of the Family

You can't expect more in your relationships with your children than you have in your relationship with each other as a couple. The two of you as a unit are the heart of the family, and unless you make each other your first priority, you'll have nothing to give your children. A lot of people get hung up on dividing their time and energy between spouse and children, even thinking that they have to somehow divide their love.

"When I think of this now, I feel so blessed and fortunate that God taught us how to be 100 percent lovers first, and it wasn't only to model for our kids, but to have more to give them. It required that we spend real quality time alone. At first, we had to do this while babies were sleeping, but it was great when they were old enough to understand and supported us being away in our room. We took time to do our dialogue of writing and sharing, making each other number one so that we would have tender, unconditional love to pass on to the kids. I shared that there were some days when I felt jealous over time that Betty gave the kids. I heard that she had postpartum blues at times, and I couldn't understand how she could possibly feel so blah when we had such a beautiful life right there in front of us until she shared. I just didn't get that Betty felt a responsibility 24 hours a day, seven days a week and knew it would never go away! That is why it was and still is so important for us to know and share each other's feelings. So many couples assume that they are feeling the same about things like this, and that often leads to stress, disillusionment, or worse. It's not always enough to just be together. When Betty and I sat and watched our children, we felt close with those heart bursts at the antics or the faces, or the googling that a baby makes, and we thought that we were having quality time. But in all reality, we were focusing on them instead of on us. When we took alone time and started sharing feelings and spending true quality time together, our good marriage became great." —Ed

The need to delve more deeply into each other's needs and reflect on your relationship is important for both you and your spouse's well-being and peace of mind. The time you spend focusing on each other is vitally important. You need to carve out time to be with each other to contemplate the purpose of your lives together. You don't have to send your kids packing to Grandma's. Little things sometimes mean more than a dozen roses and a bottle of champagne. After dinner help your wife do the dishes or help your husband with bath time. Give each other the gift of some alone time.

A compliment costs nothing. Remember that, as hard as it is to squeeze in romance and passion with kids scurrying about the house, it's worthwhile to build your relationship now so that you'll have a great marriage later on when the kids leave home and it's just the two of you.

So the next time you're too tired to take a moment with your spouse, stop for a moment and realize that it should be a priority. Make it a point to schedule some couple time to enhance the bond between the two of you. Instead of waiting for the other to make the first move, decide to be proactive about romance yourself. Think back to the activities that you found romantic before you had kids and try those same activities again whenever you can. This can be as simple as popping popcorn to watch a movie or going out to sit in the backseat of the car to have an intimate conversation! Keep one area of your house for just the two of you; for example, turn your bedroom into a romantic zone by removing all toys and other reminders of your kids and adding some romantic items, like candles or silk pillows. Make a habit of flirting with your spouse.

Me Tarzan, You Jane

Femininity and masculinity refer to the way in which we see ourselves as a man or a woman. It includes both the natural and the nurturing dimensions of sexuality. The natural component of sexuality is stamped into every cell of our bodies. The nurturing aspects of sexuality are rooted in what society thinks regarding what being male or female means. The issues and problems that surface between men and women are not just those of miscommunication or misunderstanding. Rather, one of the major challenges we face as married couples is the obscuring of our natural masculine and feminine differences. This has enormous consequences on a variety of levels. Men who have a natural abundance of masculine energies refrain from fully animating their masculinity because they've been made to believe that "real men" can't show emotion or feeling, while women who have a natural abundance of feminine energy have adopted a false masculine shell, believing that it's the only way to be powerful. They are often afraid of being called irrational or hormonal if they show their true emotions.

Each of us has masculine and feminine characteristics that need to be acknowledged. You need to appreciate and readily accept all aspects of these masculine and feminine traits, which should not be limited by our gender. It definitely is a matter of sexuality, but it is also a matter of living in balance. Due to the natural component of sexuality, men are typically aggressive and competitive and usually focus on one thing at a time, while women are passive, nurturing, expressive, and multitask easily. In striving for gender equity, which is good, our society has inadvertently squelched our appreciation and acceptance of the power of our inherent masculinity and femininity, which is the source of our true passion for each other.

"A lot of the nurturing qualities of masculinity and femininity I got by observing. I saw my grandmother grow her garden, but I saw my uncle rototill the ground. I saw my mom and grandmother cook all of the meals except barbeque. I saw Dad work and handle the big jobs like painting the house. As I got older, I watched the boys chase the girls, but the girls seemed to fish for the boys—just waiting there to catch one. I watched people shopping at the mall and saw men go in and buy while women would move from store to store shopping for the best deals. There is no doubt that my ideas of feminine and masculine characteristics were formed by observing, especially my family." —Ed

Masculinity and femininity are characteristics or tendencies that fit any male or female. However, because of the physiological differences from brain development to bodies and hormones, women tend to assume a lot of characteristics similar to other women and men assume those of other men. We then simply label the ones that women assume as feminine and the ones that men assume as masculine. The God-given reason for this is that men and women are attracted to each other precisely because of the masculine or feminine characteristics that they exude.

"The primary feminine characteristic for me is to nurture and it makes Ed and everyone in our family feel secure and loved to see me as a nurturer. For the most part, women heal hurts and make us feel invited, warm, and cuddly in the home. When I was a child, I played with dolls a lot. I even nurtured my stuffed animals. We did play cowboys and Indians too, but I can vividly remember dolls in all stages of my childhood, even to young preteen. The unisex message dished out in the 1960s and 1970s squelched

me, made me think twice about even raising children to be boy a or a girl. But I think it was an experimental time; no one knew. When we tried to make our kids unisex, it wasn't happening. Jenny was pure girl, and Tony was pure boy. That message was definitely turned around when we went to the retreat called Living in Love, and my eyes were opened to accept my sexuality, sensuality, and femininity." —Betty

Our masculine and feminine traits complement each other, just as our physical bodies are designed to do. Think of the unity candle at your wedding: two flames unite into one. One problem in our relationships today is that many of us believe that the only route is to pretend that we are not only equal, but also the same and, to some extent, even nonsexual. This false illusion keeps us ignorant, immature, unwhole, superficial, and unready for living a life of true love—human and divine. It has created a huge loss for marriages and has limited the passion and connection that result in a deeper love. Men and women's intimate relationships are becoming more and more antagonistic and troubled. This could be precisely why we have such a high divorce rate in our country.

If your masculine and feminine essence is well-balanced, you will attract, enjoy, and even prefer a spouse with an equally balanced sexual essence. For instance, you will enjoy following your partner's strong lead at times, and you will equally enjoy providing a strong lead for your partner to follow at other times. You will show concern for each other's feelings, with one partner listening and validating the other one time, and the other partner doing the same at another time without keeping score. There is no such thing as a passionate fifty-fifty proposition; each has to be invested 100 percent in a true love affair. This is the kind of relationship that will inspire love, passion, and gratitude. This is the kind of relationship that will keep the chemistry and passion between two people of the opposite sex going not just all night long, but all life long.

Is There Such a Thing as a Perfect Marriage?

Can you truly have a perfect marriage? Do Ward and June Cleaver exist in the new millennium? How many couples do you know in which the wife rushes to the door to greet her husband with a martini in one hand and his smoking jacket in the other? First, let's define *perfect*. It means without defect or blemish. Last time we checked, nobody was perfect. No marriage is without flaws. As a matter of fact, everything in nature has flaws or could improve in some way. Sooner or later, we just have to learn to find joy in an imperfect relationship.

So, are there perfect relationships? No, because there are no perfect people. Are there ideal relationships? Of course. It is much more realistic to say that your relationship is successful than that it is perfect. But how do you and your husband or wife achieve this, much less maintain a strong and lasting union? Both of you must have clarity of vision for the future as well as a true belief that God will give you what is best for you and your spouse, and you must act on that belief. Over the years, we continuously reflected on questions such as "What is our perfect relationship?" "If I could be anything I wanted, what would it be?" and "If money were no object, what would I want our life to look like?" Make a list of your dreams about how to create the perfect home. It is so important to be clear about what you both desire, and writing and brainstorming answers to these questions is the perfect way to start. However, dreaming is just that—dreaming. The next step is to pray often to be guided in the pursuit of your dreams. Our motto is "Let go and let God lead the way." If you truly put your relationship in the hands of God, He will lead you both to a loving and ideal marriage. There is a catch however; you have to listen to His words with a trusting heart. What He may have in store for your marriage may not necessarily be what either of you want or think is best. We learned along the way that it was even better than best!

"Our ideal marriage is to have a joyous, faith-filled marriage. A marriage that allows us to be free to love each other the way we want to be loved. We get to work, play, and be together all of the time. We enjoy travel, have fun, and are able to spend time with our children and grandchildren no matter where they live. Our vision is a worry-free love affair that supports us through any challenge that we may face. It has us giving to others and being generous by sharing these insights with others. Most important, however, is that we must continually pray to God for the passion for each other that will attract others to want what we have." —Ed and Betty

Do we expect our partners to be psychic and know exactly what we want? If we take some time to explore what our idea of the perfect relationship is, often we'll find things that our partner doesn't do. Unmet expectations can spiral out of control when we don't share the same vision and silently expect our spouse to know what we want. This leads to resentment and creates tension in our marriages. How many times have you been in an argument with your wife or husband and said, "I'm not a mind reader"? It is vital to create and share a common vision. Our relationship has grown tremendously by taking time to dialogue over and over about what we both envision as a perfect life together. Dialoguing and knowing yourself and then each other naturally instigates the question, "What are we going to do with this relationship?" Because of our faith, we know that we cannot keep it under a bushel basket. When you write down your idea of what an ideal relationship means to you versus what you have been experiencing, it will remind you of the direction in which you want to head. It will serve to motivate you toward experiencing your most fulfilling relationship, especially if you remember to look at it often. It is amazing what you can learn about your partner by doing this. You will find subtle nuances of his or her character that you never knew before.

A marriage is like any relationship and has its good times and bad, its agreements and disagreements. Add a couple of kids, a minivan, and a stack of bills, and those disagreements can easily turn into a meeting with a divorce lawyer and a nasty custody battle. No one can expect everything to be wonderful at every minute of the day, but you can expect your marriage to grow stronger as you overcome each obstacle. Keep your sight set on unity, not just on happiness. In many marriages, the excitement of first love tends to fade with time, but it doesn't have to. By sharing and spending quality time together, keeping your identity as a couple, and sharing your dreams, your children will be happier and your marriage will be stronger than the two of you ever could have imagined.

Chapter 1
Passionate Parents are a Passionate Couple

Passionate Points

We need to keep our relationship as husband and wife the top priority so we have something to give our children. The best ways we know to do that are Meditation and Dialogue.

Masculinity and Femininity are normal healthy physiological and psychological traits. They should be noticed, acknowledged and relished as the powerful magnets that attract, bond and draw husband and wife together.

The perfect marriage is simply one that is green and growing to become great. The worse thing you can have is a good marriage because that usually leads to settling down which becomes blah, boring and unthrilling.

Dialogue Questions

What physical, emotional and spiritual traits are most attractive about you? How does my answer make me feel?

What would our relationship be like if it were perfect, and how do I feel sharing my answer with you?

Family Meeting Sharing Questions

Since the Couple is the Heart of the family, what can I do to support and make that real in our family?

What is the most masculine trait of each of the males (boys) in our family? What is the most feminine trait of each of the females (girls) in our family?

Chapter 2
Sacred Sex

Sex and golf are the two things that you can enjoy
even if you're not good at them.

—Kevin Costner, *Tin Cup*

A trail of clothes leading to the bed. Shoes torpedo through the air and shatter the light bulb in the ceiling fan. Warm bodies against cold sheets. Bam! Five minutes later (if you're lucky), and it's time to look for the remote control. During sex, we feel so close to our spouse. Sensations run wild throughout our bodies, love overwhelms us, and we unite as one. Yes, sex is fabulous—but what happens afterward when life resumes? Why can't we stay that close throughout the normal course of our lives in both good times and bad times not just in the bedroom (or the kitchen, if you're adventurous)? Is there some way that we can maintain that connection every day, all day long?

Sex involves a lot more than learning the latest technique or wild new position. You may be an amazing contortionist or a master of the *Kama Sutra*, but these are all worthless if your relationship lacks a genuine love. Sex is only truly satisfying when it arouses your soul as well as your body. This can only be done when you and your spouse view sex in the proper context. It's largely about the connection that occurs outside the act of lovemaking itself, such as how you treat your spouse, how much you invest in your relationship, and how well you cultivate the bond that you share together. When you first realize that sex is a sacred act sanctioned by God, then you can focus on adventure and spontaneity.

In our seminars, we often hear the question, "Why is sex such a big deal in a Christian marriage?" To start with, very few human activities have as many references in the Bible as sex within marriage. Sex is one of the crucibles within which God forms and sanctifies our spiritual and emotional bond. Scripture demonstrates that the union of the sexes is God's plan for humanity. His eternal plan is to live with us in an eternal union of life and love. Because of His desire for this eternal "marital plan," He impressed an image of it in our very being by creating us male and female.

As Christians, the core of our belief is the Trinity, and God intends for marriage to be an earthly image of His own Trinitarian "exchange of love." "'For this reason a man shall leave his father and mother and be joined to his wife, and the two shall become one flesh." Sex is a real-world gift that God has given to us. Once you understand this, sex improves your mental, physical, and emotional well-being, and it brings you closer to each other and, ultimately, to God.

Sex, Sex, and More Sex

These days, you can't walk out your front door without seeing or hearing something about sex. From the little blue pill to the birth control pill, it seems that is all we hear about on TV or the radio. As the old song goes, "In olden days a glimpse of stocking was looked on as something shocking, but now, God knows, anything goes." Times may change but values don't. Two difficult challenges with which we struggle in society today are:

> Separating our expectations in the bedroom from those that we see in the media and society.

> Helping our children develop a healthy understanding of their sexuality.

Most of our training and beliefs come from what we learned from being in our family or from the culture of society, and we don't realize how influenced we are by them. The knowledge about sex that we developed in our formative years builds the foundation for our beliefs and attitudes about sex. It influences not only our lifelong pattern of sexual behavior, but also what we pass on to our children.

"My first influence about sex came from very affectionate parents, so I believed that hugs and kisses were the genuine signs of love. When Ed and I met and fell in love and words were just not adequate for expressing how I felt, I relied on my affection training. Other aspects of sex were somewhat uncomfortable until our Christian values taught me that all of that pleasure was also good for us and even holy. The influences of society seemed to get degenerately more radical and sleazy. When I slipped down that road, my beautiful Christian values got watered down. Just like the food that we ate slipped from nourishing to convenient, so, too, had our lovemaking gone from intimacy to convenience. If it was not convenient to make love in the midst of all of the other stuff we did, it just became another duty or chore." —Betty

Our parents, peers, and society play a central role in our sexuality, but there is one other major factor that many of us face today. The media influences us more than ever before. It is virtually impossible to navigate through an entire hour of any given day without being confronted with sex. Television, radio, movies, magazines, books, and the Internet are filled with almost relentless images and/or references to sex. And, as a rule, these references are not to the Godly types of sexuality. Media's role in establishing norms and expectations for people makes us ask the question, "Are we really free to love, or have we been conditioned and brainwashed into loving the way someone else thinks is best for us?" Sex has become so ingrained in our culture that what used to be outlandish is now considered ordinary. We are literally saturated with sex because it is so much a part of the media.

Our heart tells us one thing and society tells us another, so we look to society for the answer. But we know in our heart that ultimately God has the final word. So the question is who are you going to listen to—God, the world, or yourself? Sadly, what God deemed holy and special has been twisted by man to become ordinary and casual, or even shameful, degrading, and sinful.

Not Tonight, I Have a Headache—and Tomorrow Night, My Back Is Going to Hurt

Whether you and your spouse have been married for thirty years or two years, you've probably experienced a bit of the doldrums in the bedroom. You both are happier than ever and life is great, but once the lights go out, you feel like a captive in an amusement park. The rides never change and you know how they end every time. There's no fun and adventure anymore; you know what to expect. Sex has become almost robotic. This is a very bothersome scenario. Is there something missing?

If you see yourself in this situation, don't slam this book shut and run out to a marriage counselor. Let us reassure you that this is very normal, and most couples reach the stage of boredom even when they are still very much in love with each other. Couples tend to ignore this problem, hoping it will go away on its own. With this mind-set, a couple can easily wind up falling into the trap of sex becoming an activity.

Many relationships tend to lose their excitement over time, and some couples decide to spice it up a bit with sexy videos and toys. But do these types of activities enhance or destroy your love life? It is true that the short-term impact is usually enticing. In the beginning, it is arousing and acts as a type of voyeuristic foreplay, and on the surface, it seems to work. But over time, it is not enough; your relationship requires more and more. It loses its luster and becomes an insatiable need. The worst part is that it makes sex an activity, turning it into lust rather than love. Pornography fills your mind with images that detract from focusing on your spouse's true beauty, softness, tenderness, and unconditional giving.

Sex is an incredibly important part of every relationship, and for God-centered ones, bringing God into the bedroom may seem uncomfortable at first. There seems to be this myth that sex should be lights off, missionary position only, and boring. If you only take away one nugget of knowledge from this book, let it be this one: sex should be exciting, intimate, and even erotic! It is a true gift given by God and should be celebrated to the fullest and to the most enjoyable extent possible. Now, we're not talking about whips and chains or chicken feathers and fly swatters, but you can still have a good time.

"When I think of Ed and the gift of unconditional love and the beautiful children that he's given me, I know that porn and sex toys just take God out of the bedroom and reinforce the lifelong attitude that sex is dirty. We have worked so hard to make God a part of our sex life and a nonverbal expression of how much I love him when words are not enough. It's such a thrill to say something like, "I'm so thankful for this evening." Let's say a prayer by making love. When people are led down the other path, they think it will enhance their sex life, but in truth they're going through a painful, slow, destructive death, not only of their sex life, but probably of their entire marriage. I just feel so thankful and grateful that we were able to discover this. I especially feel thankful for Pope John Paul II, with his beautiful writings on Theology of the Body; *that truly helped us know, understand, and get back to being lovers, not lusters."* —Betty

Is It Love or Lust?

Intimacy between you and your spouse is a celebration both of each other and of God. A walk down the aisle to the altar doesn't give us permission to have sex anytime or in any way that we want. Marriage doesn't justify lust. When you have sex out of lust and not true genuine love, it becomes nothing more than an activity. Lust is self-centered and focuses on "what's in it for me," while love is centered on your partner and focuses on fulfilling your spouse's needs and desires. So many couples falsely believe that sex will fix what is missing in their relationship. In fact, the opposite usually occurs when sex is just for recreation or an activity. Instead of helping to bring the two of you closer, it drives an even larger wedge between you.

"For so many years, I lived with false expectations, and I was looking for sex to meet my needs and fix our relationship. It is so easy for me to see the difference, looking back now, between when I came to Betty in love versus when I came in lust. The secret for me to break out of my engrained attitude of sex being the fix-all or of sex as another activity has been for me to get out of myself long enough to look at what her needs are. Another

aspect of sex as an activity was looking for ways to spice it up, thinking that better mechanics, videos, or toys could make sex better. How silly it was to put so much emphasis on sex as an activity, forgetting the sacredness and specialness and actual wonder of sharing an open, honest love coming from my heart to hers." —Ed

What happens when sex is an activity? Passion usually dissipates slowly over the years, and a lot of times couples don't even realize it before it's already gone. Couples come to us all the time and say, "I don't know what happened or when it happened." They don't realize that the longer they remain together, the easier it is to get sidetracked and lose the true meaning of sex. Instead of communicating an ultimate sacred love, it keeps them distant from each other. Sex becomes impersonal and shallow and, more often than not, most people feel used and ask themselves, "Is this all there is?"

"At first I thought it was just adventuresome and fun trying new things and focusing on the pleasure and fun. But over time, approaching sex as an activity took its toll. Doing 'it' became more and more prominent. Then achieving satisfaction got stronger. I got totally self-centered: my love got less and less, and my heart got harder and harder. I felt blue and longing because I forgot what love was. I still feel numb and without feeling when I think about how it had become." —Betty

As expressed by Christopher West in *Theology of the Body for Beginners,* the body has a "language" that is meant to image God's free, total, faithful, fruitful love. For sex to be sacred, what our body is saying has to be connected to what our mind and heart are saying. When our mind and heart are saying, "I want to be committed to you alone for the rest of my life" (free, faithful), "I can't express in words how close I want to be with you" (total), and "I am open to creating life and making you my first priority" (fruitful); then our body language and heart are aligned and sex becomes sacred.

This sacred body language that prevents our union from being an activity is the key to keeping our intimacy from becoming rote and boring. When you and your spouse dwell on this rather than just sex, you'll touch physically and spiritually in the purest and kindest way. Sex as sacred body language also means holy and blessed. We truly experience this in our faithfulness to the practice of skin to skin when we lie naked in each other's arms for twenty minutes and choose to just be sensuous, tender, and touching without the expectation of intercourse.

Focusing on this sacred body language is the solution and solving of the riddle: how do we keep our lovemaking from being self-centered and just an activity? When we focus on phrases such as "the two shall become one," "or two in one flesh," we are unified in mind, body, and spirit during our lovemaking.

While sex as lust or activity will lead to separation, sacred sex has a body language that allows us to strengthen our bond with not only each other but with God as well. As a result, sex is enhanced far beyond society's concept of marriage. With this practice, the bond between the two of you is permanently cemented and your experience of genuine love and sacred sex turns into a celebration of not only your own special connection, but also your connection with God.

"I want sex to be sacred body language for me. For several years, I had slipped into seeing sex as an activity and had become very self-centered. When we finally understood that we had been using each other and that sex had become lust and not love, it took a very special experience in a hotel room while we were on vacation to break us out of the trap that we were in. It is now much easier to recreate this feeling by recalling glimpses of the experience in which we decided to not touch each other until we knew that it was love and not lust driving us. While we were lying side by side, there were times when I was conscious of Betty's specialness to me, and I would be seeing her as a gift from God. Then thoughts of 'what's in it for me?' would slip in. This long-engrained attitude kept popping into my mind. It's almost like I needed a prayerful ritual to keep me holy. We waffled back and forth between lust and love for what seemed like an eternity, although it was not even an hour. Finally, we were able to focus completely on the other, and miracles happened. Now I strive to love Betty in that way, to show her desirability, to make our lovemaking a prayer. Media all around us makes lust without love seem so right. I feel so hollow at times when I realize how I fall into this trap. However, I know that we have done it, and I know that by God's grace we can continue to make our lovemaking a true expression of love with God in the heart of it." —Ed

The amazing and hugely positive aspect to remember is that changing your perspective from sex as an activity to a celebration of your love is one of the most powerfully intimate experiences that exists. When we don't focus on each other and have sex out of lust rather than love, the intimate bond between man and wife is lost, and inevitably a sense of emptiness finds its way into our marriage. With sacred sex, you and your spouse will experience all of the blessings that God has to offer. Lust is a poor substitute for true genuine love, and if you and your husband or wife are experiencing sex as God intended, you will find that you, your marriage, and your family will all benefit.

Remember When We Could Stand to Be in the Same Room with Each Other?

How can we maintain the feelings that we had for each other when we were dating? The best technique for us was the use of natural family planning (NFP). It's allowed us to experience a continuous courtship and honeymoon throughout our passionate marriage instead of just one time! The idea behind natural family planning is very simple. Sperm live a maximum of five days, and the ovum lives only 24 hours once released, so there are very few days when intercourse has a chance to result in pregnancy. Those wanting to avoid pregnancy refrain from sexual intimacy during the window of fertility. This also becomes the life-giving time for renewing our love by recreating courtship and romance. In our early days of NFP, we thought that the fertile time was a time of separation and hands-off, which actually put a strain on our relationship. But after we shifted our attitude to making this a time of "dating," it became adventuresome and exciting. One powerful source for how to stay connected without sex was from Gary Chapman's book and its five love languages, which are words, touch, deeds, gifts, and physical presence. The key is to use this time of abstinence to find out what your spouse's preferred love language is. Then when we become infertile, it is like experiencing our honeymoon over and over in every fertility cycle. Although natural family planning, is as effective as the most popular methods of contraception, we don't consider it to be only a method of birth control.

Is natural family planning for everyone or just for religious fanatics and health freaks? Can you believe that many couples actually find that periodic abstinence is beneficial rather than harmful to their marriage? Now please don't misunderstand us; abstinence can at times be difficult, especially on a cold winter night when you're snuggling under the covers, but it also brings its benefits. Many of our students at first have a difficult time understanding how this type of restraint is beneficial. We like to use the diet analogy. If you want to lose twenty pounds, you have to refrain from eating certain foods. We're not nutritionists, but it doesn't take a rocket scientist to figure out that you won't lose weight if you guzzle Dr. Pepper and stuff your face with Oreos every day. You have to change your mind-set and limit the times you eat unhealthy and fattening foods. The end result of fitting into your skinny jeans or favorite outfit far outweighs the sacrifices that you have made. The same is true with abstinence and natural family planning.

Natural family planning gives you and your spouse the opportunity to communicate your affection in other ways. By refraining from intercourse, the two of you are able to recapture those feelings that you felt before marriage. Romance reenters the relationship during the times of abstinence as each of you experiences the anticipation and excitement of having intercourse again when you are in the infertile times.

"Why is natural family planning important? When using contraception, I would come home from work and, as I started to kiss and tease Betty, she immediately felt, 'Oh, I have to put out tonight.' She felt used and could not trust my motives. But when we were using natural family planning, we both knew the times that we would be abstaining and could possibly get pregnant. During the times of abstinence when I came home and I hugged and kissed and teased her, she really knew that it was because of my love for her and not just because I wanted something. This increased her trust and carried over to the times that we could make love. When we used contraception, all of that magical time disappeared and it just became so obvious how difficult it is to really communicate true love. I think that natural family planning just really helps us to better live our marriage vows by knowing that we are being faithful, free, total, and life-giving as we make love to each other." —Ed

With natural family planning, you and your husband or wife will also experience a greater bond not only with each other but also with God. Spouses using this method find that they come to understand and respect one another more. They feel like they are not only removing some of their own barriers but also opening themselves more to union with God. God is the source of love and life, and He has privileged us with the transmitters of life through the act of love.

"Being aware of your fertility is exciting, natural, earthy, basic and knowledgeable, and it makes you so much more complete as a person. Is contraception the elephant in the room? Is he sitting there waiting to take away your heartfelt love? I feel complete, secure, intelligent, all-encompassing. It's like having this most wonderful secret to share with people. You trust me, don't you? You want to have a lifelong love affair, don't you? Then listen to this!" —Betty

Having sacred sex is a very important component of a couple's marriage, and it's also one of the most difficult to maintain in the long term. Couples frequently struggle with this issue because they often fall into the trap of viewing sex as an activity and don't understand why the passion dwindles or how to recreate their holy union. Many people aren't even aware of what is missing from their relationship. They know that something is wrong, but they just can't put their finger on it.

Sex powered by lust is unfulfilling and dissatisfying. It eventually fails to incite desire and arousal and leads to feelings of alienation, being used, and mistrust. Instead of looking forward to falling into each other's arms, couples feel like it's an obligation or duty and begin to avoid one another. Over time, the marriage relationship erodes, and soon they find that they are just going through the motions.

Sacred sex, however, brings a couple closer together physically, emotionally, and spiritually. It enhances the quality of the relationship on all levels. Not only are both you and your spouse more content, satisfied, and happy with your relationship, but life in general is more fulfilling. The most important point to remember is that sacred sex in a marriage requires commitment, understanding, and honest communication.

Chapter 2
Sacred Sex

Passionate Points

Most of our attitudes about sex were formed through the influence of our family, street talk from peers and especially media in our society. By and large these attitudes have lead to a 50% divorce rate, so isn't it time to see if there is something better?

Love is a gift of self while lust is using the other, which is self-centered. To have sacred sex requires that what our body is saying has to be connected to what our mind and heart are saying.

To keep your relationship vibrant the best mentality is to continuously date each other with the freshness, excitement, and adventure that you had before marriage. Natural Family Planning actually gave us the perfect opportunity to experience a time of courtship and honeymoon in every fertility cycle.

Dialogue Questions

How do I feel when I think about sex as being sacred?

What am I willing to do to make sure our sexual relationship stays other centered? How do I feel sharing this with you?

Family Meeting Sharing Questions

What makes a person ugly to me?

What makes a person beautiful to me?

Chapter 3
Modeling

Don't try to make children grow up to be like you, or they may do it.

—Russell Baker

A baby is a precious gift. From the moment they lay him or her in your arms, you've fallen head over heels in love, and after the first time that baby wraps his or her little hand around your finger, your life will never be the same. We only think we know the true meaning of love until we have our first child. Our babies depend on us parents for everything that they need. It is our privilege to provide them with love, care, attention, food, and shelter. When we become parents, we take on an entirely different role in our lives.

Nobody teaches us to be parents. There isn't any manual that comes with these little bundles of joy. All we wanted to do was to love our kids, but we didn't realize that love included discipline, boundaries, consequences, rewards, and our ability to adjust to change frequently. Many times in our lives, we found ourselves on our knees praying for a time machine to take us from the teenage years back to the toddler years. Looking back, we were so dense. We always said that we were two college-educated people and should be able to figure this out. However, college is not the answer for being great parents. We were consumed and overwhelmed, and the kids were running us ragged. We saw everything that we didn't like in them as problems that the kids were having. We could not connect that the kids were reacting to the way we were behaving and how we treated them. We did not say what we meant. We would say, "Stop doing that," but did nothing to enforce it other than repeating the command a hundred times more. We had no guidelines or consequences set up, and we were totally operating from the seat of our pants, hoping that things would just work out automatically. We slowly learned that that just doesn't happen.

Why does it take so long for us as parents to realize that we have to be clear about what we want and that it is up to us to give clear messages to our children? We have six children, and over the years, we had to learn that getting angry and yelling wasn't going to modify their behavior. Screaming only gives you a headache and makes matters worse. It is our responsibility as parents to instill a sense of self-discipline, self-motivation, and self-love in our children, and that will happen when we live what we want in them. We brought them into this world, but we don't have the right to take them out of it, no matter how tough things get! We owe it to them to be their good role model.

Oh My God, I'm Turning into My Mother

We can vividly remember as newlyweds discussing children and how we would raise them. Our first reaction was that we were definitely not going to be like our parents. Little did we know that those words would soon come back to haunt us. Earaches in the middle of the night, potty training, and a general overall sense of cluelessness had us reaching for the phone to call our parents more than once. We discovered that our natural style of parenting was caught by observing our parents and our culture. Many of our personality traits are passed on to our kids at a very early age. In one of our seminars, we met a couple who were polar opposites. Lynn was a huge germophobe, while Chris had no problem eating food out of the dumpster. As we talked to them about the way that they wanted to raise their first child, he immediately said, "I don't want Sara to be raised like you were. Promise me that you won't make her afraid to walk barefoot in a hotel room like your mother did to you."

The longer we visited with this couple, the more we learned about each of them. He came from a big family in which the definition of a clean house meant that floors were mopped annually and the potato chips under the couch were still edible. She, on the other hand, was raised in a home that resembled a DuPont test lab for plastic. Every surface with the exception of the toilet, according to Chris, was covered so that it would be kept clean. Obviously, Lynn and Chris came from totally different backgrounds, and there were some issues as to how they were going to raise their baby. They had a lot of work to do in coming to a consensus on what they wanted to model as parents; otherwise they would be continuously sending mixed messages to their children.

"One of the things I caught by observing my parents and wanted to avoid was being a special-events dad. I didn't want to be the dad that just showed up a few times or took kids out on a special treat day. I wanted my kids to know that I was involved in parenting on a daily basis. Another thing that I observed and hoped would be true in our marriage was how moms seemed to know how to fix hurts. I thought that was a very good trait. I had never been trained medically, and I knew Betty wasn't trained either, so it is odd how I still expected her to know how to handle that part of child raising. It is amazing how I put the burden on her for what to do psychologically as well as physiologically when the kids were hurting." —Ed

Culture also plays a great role in our modeling as we raise our children. Ideally, it would be nice to ignore what others in the world do, but sometimes the peer pressure is too difficult, and as parents we follow the flock and raise our kids according to culture's rules rather than our own.

"One thing that I got from our culture had to do with the equal rights movement, which I misinterpreted. I was confused and thought that I wanted boys and girls to be the same, and I was self-conscious about staying at home and not being a career woman. As I became more confident about what I wanted in my life, I made conscious choices about which of society's ideas I would keep and which ones I would discard. What I would keep was having the American dream—being free to choose anything I wanted in life.

I would discard what I learned in the instant gratification mode about not saving up for things and being impatient. I would discard how I was taught to downplay masculinity and femininity. I would discard the idea that sex is dirty and the concept that if it feels good, do it. I would also discard the concept of sex as activity and would cherish the beauty of sex." —Betty

If you have noticed, most children imitate their parents; therefore, by not setting a good example as a role model, you're encouraging certain types of behavior. The most successful parents are the ones who see the importance of role modeling and come to grips with what they want to model. They can ignore what others think and say and spend quality time with their kids when their neighbor might be working overtime for a new car. They can choose to chat with their children daily, teaching them good from bad, and can correct them when they do something wrong—or, more importantly, catch them doing something right! They are present for teachable moments and experience the opportunity to instill manners, moral values, how to share, and respect for others. The only way to make this behavior attractive and believable for our children is to live these same behaviors ourselves.

I'm Not Afraid of Change; Just Yesterday I Changed the Channel on TV

Change is one of the fundamental keys of life. As with any living thing in nature, if we don't change, we don't grow, and inevitably, we die. But there is a catch: you can't change others, no matter how hard you may try. Some of us go into a marriage thinking that there are certain qualities or characteristics that we can change about our spouse. Not a good idea! The truth is that you can only change yourself. Change has been significant in our lives, especially in regard to our relationship. After a Worldwide Marriage Encounter Weekend, we knew that we loved each other for who we were, not just for who we wanted each other to become. Then both of us were able to look at the circumstances and situations that affected our relationship and decided to change for the sake of us. It was very empowering and freeing to not feel manipulated. We had open communication to express how we felt, and we wanted to change for each other.

With our kids it was the same. We wanted cooperation from them, but then we realized that we were not willing to do so ourselves. It was a constant battle, because we felt like we had to be in control all the time. It wasn't, however, until deciding to mellow out, give up control, and set up guidelines with nonpunitive consequences that cooperation was really born. Our change allowed the children to change.

To have a better relationship with your spouse or children, you can't just wait around for everyone else around you to change. If you are not in control of your life, your life will be in control of you. So take a moment and ask yourself what it is that you need to change about yourself to have a better relationship with your husband, wife, or family. Are there certain habits or routines that you need to break, creating better ones in their place?

Your willingness to change is a very important part of you being able to have fulfilled relationships. Change will always be necessary as long as you strive to live a happier life with your loved ones. So just make the decision right now that you will be willing to change whatever is necessary without losing your integrity. If you do, a better marriage and family will be the result for you.

"It was a big shock to hear on the Marriage Encounter Weekend that I can only change myself, and to believe that if I do, Ed and our children will eventually want to do the same. I know that if we share feelings, especially of hurt or sadness, the others in the love relationships will want to change. The best times for sharing these difficult feelings might be in family meetings or dialogue. Like when I shared with Ed about how I want to run away when he gets angry, and he listened so intently that he seemed to share my feeling. I felt so loved when he shared so earnestly that he wanted to stop that behavior. It made me feel so much closer to him. There are so many questions sometimes. What if you don't remember what you said? What if you didn't mean it? What if I don't deserve your love? What if I don't keep my side of the bargain and stay changed for you? But these are all of the things that come up because of the trust being broken and needing to be rebuilt. Making changes for each other is a process that will continue forever." —Betty

Change is a difficult process on its own, and when you or members of your family don't offer support and show mutual respect and trust for each other, it is almost impossible. What if we told you that mutual respect and trust can't be earned, because we are all human and can let each other down? Instead, these are gifts and decisions. Mutual respect and trust speak of relationship, yet the decision to do so can at times seem like a calculated move to get something you want in return. A tit for tat, if you will. However, when we consider these a gift, we don't want anything in return. These are just key ingredients that help modeling parents provide a fantastic experience for their children. We want to change to be better for each other when we live with cooperation as the foundation. But we are human, which means that we are growing, which means that we will let each other down. We will make mistakes along the way. At that point, we have two choices: (1) Give up on each other, go our separate ways, and say things like "I knew you didn't care about me." Or (2) we can share, ask forgiveness, heal, and start over. Decisions and gifts are lived out, and we continue to strive for mutual respect and trust.

"I know that I have broken promises, made mistakes, lied, and done so many more things that have provided reasons for Betty to not trust me, yet she forgives and allows me the privilege of starting over again and again. She decides to give me the gift of trust. That's how I know that it can't be earned, because I know in my heart that I don't deserve it, and yet Betty blesses me with it. In our parenting, I think we showed unconditional trust and respect, and because of that I think we knew a lot more about what our kids were doing than most parents know. I think we were clear that we just wanted them to be able to be honest and that we were willing to start anew no matter what it was that they had or hadn't done. Some of the things that our kids did were funny, like eating all of the candy that we were supposed to be selling for the baseball team's fundraiser or hiding the newspaper inserts under the house so that it would be easier to deliver the newspapers. These have subsequently become lifelong lessons and even family jokes. But all of these things helped us to understand trust as a decision made by the other. It is so important in a family to be able to know that as a human you will make mistakes, but that others will give you a chance to start over. That's the decision to trust. It is core to building a close family." —Ed

Knowing you can't change others is vital to parenting. This realization is huge. Ultimately, by changing yourself and then sharing your expectations and dreams and caring for each other, your spouse or children will want to change for you. This is why dialoguing is so important for us as a couple, and sharing in family meetings is so important for the children. These sharing times let us reveal what we envision, but ultimately we have to let go and let the others be themselves. At times it takes lots of patience; it's like planting seeds and waiting for the sprouts to appear.

How can you set yourself up for success as a parent, and is it possible to know how, when, and where to get help without feeling like a failure? It's simple: it's a matter of not taking kids' behavior as a reflection on you. We all know great parents who had so-called bad kids and bad parents who had great kids. One definition of insanity is to do the same thing over and over and expect different results. So all you need to do is something different. Don't wait too long. When kids have low self-esteem and are losing confidence in themselves and in you as a parent, it is getting too late. Try a parenting class at your child's school like we did at Ho'ala School. If this is not available, look up parenting classes online. The ability to ask and accept help without feeling like a failure is a sign of maturity. Change is hard enough, so it's okay to get support from friends, classes, and members of organizations who believe like you do.

Love Is Unconditional until They Wreck Your Car

"For better or worse, through sickness and in health." No, we're not talking about wedding vows; we're actually talking about our children. The hospital staff should make you and your spouse repeat these words before you take your newborn home. As parents of six children, we know firsthand that there will be good and bad times as well as several thousand trips to the pediatrician's office. Kids can drive us stark raving mad, and the very next moment they can melt our hearts. Anyone with a sixteen-year-old child learning how to drive a car with a standard transmission for the first time knows the meaning of unconditional love. Mistakes are part of the everyday life of a child, and it is our job to teach them that it's okay and that you love them no matter what.

Most parenting skills are based on working on yourself and becoming who you want to be and who you want your children to see. There is no such thing as "do what I say, not what I do." Don't do what you don't want to see in your children. It is so important to live your word. If you commit to something, do it. If you agree to something, really agree. Don't just give lip service. It is better to be silent than to make off-handed comments that you have no intention of honoring. If someone asked us if we planned to attend a certain event, we used to say "yes" just to appease the person and end the conversation. Since we had no idea whether or not we really intended to go, this was not in keeping with our integrity and often led to broken trust and damaged relationships. If parents are flexible and adapt their role as their child grows, they will encourage their child to flourish and become an independent, well-adjusted adult, which is our ultimate parenting goal. We know what you're thinking: "Flexible, yeah right, how can I be flexible when they stay out all night and I've got to get up for work the next morning?" The key is unconditional love.

A parent's unconditional love is a decision that is the most important part of a child's life. Unconditional means complete and absolute, and not dependent on certain terms or conditions. No matter what that child does, the parents will still love him or her with every part of their soul and with every beat of their heart. A love for a child is unlike any other love that you could ever have in your life. It is different from the love that you have for a parent or a friend or a family member. This kind of love is the soul's recognition of the closest feeling to Heaven that you can get without dying. We believe that God gives us children so that we may love another person the way that He loves us. It truly is unexplainable in words. The only way to really understand this love is to experience it.

"Unconditional love is discipline and following through and not reacting in anger. It is separating what the child does from who the child is. It requires that we get in touch with our own expectations, which may not be the same as those of our children. We love them where they are at and gently encourage them. We set goals with them in charge instead of telling them what their goals should be. Being a successful parent means modeling and instilling a desire in your child to want to be an unconditional lover." —Betty

If unconditional love is a decision, how do I live that out in our parenting? Unconditional love is easiest to understand when you see the opposite. Some examples include when people track how much time you spend with someone else versus how much time you spend with them, or when they keep score and say things like, "I do so much for you, and you do nothing for me." For us there were three keys to making unconditional love real in our lives. First of all, it emanated from our home-is-a-refuge attitude. This meant no criticism, no belittling, no excessive teasing, and no roughness. It was always safe to be in our home no matter what you did. Our kids knew how much we loved them no matter how bad they felt something was. Second, it was important to distinguish between not liking their actions or words versus not liking them. Third, and the best thing we learned, was to listen and figure out the feelings behind the words rather than to only pay attention to the words themselves.

"After lots of practice, I finally got that when children say, 'I hate you,' they are really saying, 'I'm feeling hurt, sad, angry,' or some other feeling that's going on inside based on the situation. It is hard for me to express my own feelings, so it is not surprising that a child doesn't have the words to express what is going on inside and simply lets it out in a way that may not seem clear to the parent. I learned to hear the feelings and then repeat back, 'you must be feeling very hurt, sad, or angry right now,' instead of hearing the words 'I hate you' and taking it as disrespect. That's when I really started understanding unconditional love. I think that parents who get hung up on the words and get into shouting matches and get into the whole defensive arena of feeling disrespected miss a tremendous opportunity to demonstrate not only unconditional love but also a totally mature understanding of feelings." —Ed

Parenting takes a lot of patience and practice. A five–year-old, for example, takes at least 36 hours longer to do a simple task than the average adult takes to do the same task. And for some reason, their decisions to become independent and do it themselves seem to always happen at a time when you are running late. At times, we may just want to rip our hair out and scream, "I'm late; let me tie your shoes!" So many things about being a parent fall under the true meaning of love. Children take longer to understand and learn for obvious reasons as they process life's lessons.

Remember that falls, bruises, and tears are all part of childhood, but if kids know that there is unconditional love waiting for them at home, then everything is going to be all right.

Don't Plant a Pumpkin Expecting a Daisy

How is "you reap what you sow" important in parenting when you realize that you definitely reap what you sow? One day at the mall, we heard a man yelling at his children to be quiet. What do you think he was teaching them? He was teaching them to yell in order to get what they want. Our kids are like sponges, absorbing everything we say and do and then imitating our actions. Life with a family is a magnificent adventure—not simply a hassle, filled with laundry and dishes. Remind yourself of this as often as necessary—in other words, constantly.

If you want your kids to be healthy, fit, kind, and compassionate, you'll need to live that way, too. Treat your mind, body, and soul with the utmost respect. Model caring, kindness, and compassion by working together as a family on a volunteer or church project for a few hours a month. Strive to be honest, open, and attentive with your spouse and kids. When your children are speaking, get down on their level, ask questions, and really listen to their point of view.

Work with your child on mistakes in a respectful way. Never criticize, especially in front of other adults or children, including siblings. Strive to understand their unique point of view. Taking the time to do so sends a message that you accept and trust their decisions and that their opinions are valuable and important. A major way to improve a child's self-esteem is to take him or her seriously.

Labeling your children is detrimental even when those labels sound harmless. Words aren't the only way to label a child either; the power of thought can also be used to label a child as slow or weak scholastically, or good in athletics, or whatever. People, including parents, push those labels on a child, and the child performs exactly up to those expectations. Adages like "the power of intention," "to think is to create," "be careful what you wish for," and all of those types of statements have to do with thought and how thought is the first step in the creative process. We have experienced so often the power of thought and the transformations that it has allowed our children to make just by changing our own thinking about them or their situation. Keep not only your words but also your thoughts positive.

The bottom line is to make sure that our thinking is focused positively on what we really want and encourage the kids through positive expectations. Don't go down the slippery slope of allowing yourself or others, including teachers, to put handicapping labels on any child. We must all realize that we live our life to the best of our ability (usually) and that others are affected by how we are being. The messages that we are putting out either verbally or nonverbally are being accepted or rejected by those around us. Whether it's labeling and putting things out into the universe that come back in karma, or it's saying something within earshot of the child or children, thinking that they are deaf—it's an absolute no-no. We should always respect the person that they are and the adult they are becoming while respecting all of the stages that they will go through to get there.

Accentuate the Positive

Take advantage of any negative events or situations that you see in daily life—for example, at the grocery store or at the movies or on TV—and turn them into positive things. These provide opportunities to sit down and discuss what's going on and what you and your family can learn from them. This is critical so that not all life lessons have to be learned firsthand. When a family is arguing in the store, or when something from a movie or TV shows disrespect, hurtfulness, poor judgment, or some value that we don't promote, it is the perfect chance to discuss what is wrong and decide with your child what would have been better. If the child observes these things without the parent's input, he or she could misinterpret and form faulty opinions based on limited experiences and his or her own perception. So adult supervision is critical. Children must be guided through the real world so that they'll know how to handle situations on their own in later life.

"For me, some of the best teachable moments included (1) Treating each church event, such as baptism, first communion, confirmation, and weddings, as an occasion for a huge faith and family celebration. (2) Modeling going to retreats, etc. as an important thing to do in your life's journey. (3) Visiting and going to churches all over the United States and the world whenever on trips and vacation so that the kids can see that lots of people do have faith. (4) Praying and offering difficult moments up to God in everyday life. (5) Nighttime prayers, mostly done by the dad in our family to give him a special 'moment in time' with each child at this wonderfully vulnerable time." — Betty

With our children, we used these teachable moments to give them valuable life lessons. This helped them to see the need to set clear guidelines as well as the consequences for stepping over them, allowing our children to see both sides of a situation. Another important teachable moment for our children was night prayers. We would go to each child's bed to give him or her a special one-on-one moment. The sleepiness and vulnerability made it easy to let go of the day's busyness, adventures, frustrations, hurts, anger, resentment, or whatever. It allowed both of us, parent and child, the opportunity to say "I'm sorry" and to grant forgiveness and provided us all with a clean slate for a good night's sleep filled with love. Another important part of being positive is how we shared our faith in our prayer time as a family. Our prayer—"Lord, may others be drawn to you by the way they see us living and loving in our lives"—kept us focused on being an attractive family. We lived our faith and included our children as a vital part of it, not just as spectators. Our experiences became theirs. It's a true blessing and joy to realize that there is a love of faith that we've been able to transmit to all of our children.

"We were living in a three-bedroom, one-bath, 910-square-foot house, with six kids who slept on futons across the floor of one bedroom. I know that some of the kids did not have faith when we did our butcher-paper dream sheets where they dreamed about having their own bedrooms. We all saw the dream come true, and none of us, including me, knew how or where the money would come from. How we ever remodeled the house into a six-bedroom, three-bath, almost-4000-square-foot mansion is almost a miracle!" —Ed

Chapter 3
Modeling

Passionate Points

You must be able to live and make real in your lives as a parent anything you want from your children. You have the maturity and committed relationship which is the perfect place to test anything. If you can't do it, don't expect your kids to do it! You can't change others only yourself.

Mutual respect and trust cannot be earned because we are all human and will let each other down. These important qualities of relationship require unconditional love which is a decision and a gift.

Take advantage of the negative things that your family observes in others, TV, movies, etc., as teachable moments, so that every lesson does not have to be learned the hard way.

Dialogue Questions

What behavior do I dislike in our child (children), and what am I willing to change in myself to make a difference? How do I feel sharing this with you?

How can I be a passionate lover to you and a responsible parent for our children at the same time? How do I feel about my answer?

Family Meeting Sharing Questions

What makes me feel safe and secure in our home?

When somebody says something bad about me, how does it make me feel and what do I want to do about it?

Chapter 4
Feelings and Humor

*It's not what I do, but the way I do it. It's not
what I say, but the way I say it.*

—Mae West

Research studies show that a sense of humor can add an additional eight years to your life! And that's no joke (get it?). Laughter can also keep us mentally healthy and can even cure cancer, heart disease, and many stress-related illnesses. Humor produces several positive effects on your physical, mental, and emotional well-being. So, not only do you stand to increase the potential length of your life, but you certainly increase the quality and enjoyment of it. Humor has many different definitions for people. Some think that videos of men getting smacked in the crotch by their son with a baseball bat are hilarious (we personally think most that find this funny are women). Others find bodily functions entertaining. There are even people who think mimes are funny. It takes all kinds of activities to make us laugh. So, why do we want to laugh? It's simple—because it makes us feel better.

When we think of the impact of humor, our son, Tony, is the first person in our family who comes to mind. For some reason, some people like him are magnets of humor. He somehow adds humor to just about everything with a witty play on words that makes you laugh. He's not really a joke teller, but he can keep the mood light and fun. At the lunch table, Danny had a piece of food on his cheek. Tony, from the other side of the table, motioned for Danny to wipe it off by touching his own cheek. Of course Danny wiped the wrong side of his face, and instead of correcting, Tony just said, "You got it," and moved on as though everything was fine. The rest of us could not contain our laughter, imagining Danny going through the day with food on his face.

We can't imagine surviving the stress of life without a sense of humor. Whenever it has been a while without a good belly laugh, we really notice the relief and peace that follows when the laugh finally comes. It's important to make humor a very big part of every family. Have you ever been in an argument with one of your family members when something makes the two of you laugh? Humor has the innate ability to make us forget our problems and look at life with a new perspective. In our family, humor plays a very large part. Humor, jokes, and games are great ways to diffuse any anger and pain when used correctly and with compassion. A great trigger for times of humor and breaking tension revolve around lines from our favorite family movies. Specifically, *The Jerk* with Steve Martin and *The Three Amigos* with Steve Martin, Martin Short, and Chevy Chase are two of our favorites. "This is all I need … my lamp shade," "Don't stand near the cans," "Let's just have fun with it," "Could it be that you are angry about something else, El Guapo?" "Lip balm, anyone?" If you have not seen these movies, then these lines would not mean as much, but bringing these images up at the right time in a difficult situation can immediately shake us out of the doldrums and get us back on the mend.

We have some friends who were living in their Airstream while they were building a house. The close quarters got to Donna after a while, and this seemingly normal and sane housewife morphed into Mr. Hyde from Dr. Jekyll. One evening the trailer got the best of her, and she tore into her husband, Murray, like a crazed lunatic. After he fell to the fetal position, making every attempt to shield himself from Donna's screams, their brown lab, Cosmo, cut one. Now, if you've been in any travel trailer, you know that there isn't much room for odor to disperse. Well, the two of them fell apart laughing and forgot what the fight was even about. Laughter permits us to cope with the harsh reality of living, sharing, loving, arguing, and learning, allowing us a smiling attitude toward our spouse and family.

A great sense of humor begins with a choice of attitude. Commit to look for at least one "family funny" each day, and you will find it. Share it with your spouse or kids. Before you know it, you will be surrounded by a greater sense of humor and equipped with the resilience that you need in order to cope in those not-so-funny moments. Just start looking and listening for the family funny in your everyday life. Each time that you and your brood are faced with a fight over who gets the car Friday night or because Susie borrowed Sally's sweater without asking, think to yourself, "How could I use humor to lighten up or diffuse this intense situation? Would this be funny if it were happening to someone else? Will I think this is funny later?" Or use your imagination: "Wouldn't it have been funny if …?"

Say Hi to the Boogieman for Me

In order to keep our sanity, we did many little things that we relished as private jokes between the two of us, things we could fall back on from time to time just to get the laugh and the giggle that we needed to survive as parents. One of our favorites was "Say 'hi' to the boogieman". At the time, we lived in a very dark area in a house that was up near a forest reserve that had no streetlights and a mailbox that was way out at the end of the driveway, probably about 75 feet from the house. We would be inside and suggest that someone should go get the mail. One of our brave little kids would ante up and say, "I'll do it," and start out the door, going down the long, dark way to the mailbox toward the forest. When they got far enough away, under our breath we would simply whisper, "Say 'hi' to the boogieman for me." Now, we're not mean, and the kids couldn't even hear that we had said it. It was just what we imagined would have happened if they did hear when they were halfway down the driveway and what they might have done—freaking out and coming back to the house—that gave us such a big laugh. So this became a usual thing that we did when we sent kids into a scary situation, and we would just turn to each other and say under our breaths, "Say 'hi' to the boogieman for me." It was just our cute way of maintaining sanity, keeping levity and happiness in our lives as we raised these beautiful children to be brave and resilient.

A strong sense of humor gets relationships past the uncomfortable moments and builds ease of companionship. When a speaker is presenting to an audience that he doesn't know, he will often open with a joke or funny story as an icebreaker. It gets the people relaxed and on his side. So, too, in a couple and in a family, the jokes that happen and are carried on as memories soften the barriers that might be there or come up. Why? It's easier to catch a fly with honey than with vinegar, and a sense of humor is in the honey category (although we don't know why you would want to catch a fly). It makes it so much easier to listen when the delivery is light-hearted and fun. Just a tiny word of caution though: being funny when a hurtful situation arises doesn't work, because it could communicate a lack of caring. Humor helps us as parents to facilitate communication and build relationships with our children.

When we think about us, we use humor all the time. We love the bantering at the beginning of our family meetings during opening shares. The comments that people make about how they "love" Danny's beeping watch for time keeping; the laughter and jokes that go around help keep the mood light for sharing to happen. Even intense and uncomfortable situations can later become a family joke. One example is how significant others had to fight their way into our family. We pity the young man or woman who tried to be good enough for any of the siblings and was on the hot seat at one of our family meetings! It's so great to see how they look back on the situation and now see it as humorous and look forward to watching the experience of the next victim.

"A comic relief that I use is "make-believe food or drink" in the car. When the kids start to complain about being hungry or thirsty, I push a button near the front of the console and pretend that I'm filling a cup, ask them what flavor they want, make up any kind of food that they want, and everyone pretends to taste how good it is. The other night, even our 18-month-old grandson, Elijah, was partaking, and it was just so funny to watch him wonder if he would really taste something or not. I mean, he's not even two and already knows how to pretend." —Ed

From our experience, we know that our shared jokes, games, stories, and anecdotes helped us to become closer with each other. Family environments in which humor is supported develop a culture that utilizes the humor to reduce stress and provide perspective. Learning to laugh at ourselves and at our mistakes lightens the load. One of the best opportunities for light-hearted fun and humor is playing games together. It can be kickball, charades, cards, or board games; any of these provide chances for laughter and happy interaction between children of all ages.

Humor is a major asset within a family that shouldn't be overlooked, so let's be serious about humor and use it to lighten our seriousness in the household. Laughter provides a nonthreatening medium through which a parent or child can communicate with others without intensifying the emotional temperature of the situation. Jokes and laughter take the seriousness out of a tense moment and provide us with the opportunity to become more connected with each other.

"Sharing and reliving old memories is important to bring closeness and unity. All we have to do is picture our family after someone has recited a line from Three Amigos. *There are giggles and touching and knowing glances. It's a beautiful thing—the joy, the laughter, and the true happiness it brings. It's a belonging and bonding occasion. I think, also, that photos are important. Even thinking of the picture of Chrysy on her Strawberry Shortcake bicycle wearing her rainbow backpack and her Strawberry Shortcake bathing suit and her red boots makes me smile. Show that to anyone in the family, and they get sweet feelings of camaraderie. Memories, especially comical ones, just can't be beat. The family that laughs together stays close forever.* —Betty

When the Laughter Stops

It is important to be aware of feelings for each individual in the family, from toddler to grandparent, because they control our inner being so much. So, we can't laugh at everything. We need to take into account the way our spouse or another family member feels before reacting. Feelings are neither right nor wrong and can't be judged. They just pop up based on the situation or on our attitude in relation to the moment. But, nevertheless, feelings can't be controlled. Opinions and judgments are conscious thoughts that we decide to make based on what we have caught from life or what we have been taught by others or by our life experiences.

They are based on our values and ideals. All of these things together tell us a lot about the person, but the feelings reveal our personal uniqueness. The feelings inside answer the question, "Who am I, right now, this very minute?" It is important to understand the difference between sharing feelings versus sharing opinions and judgments in order to create closeness and intimacy.

People often start off by saying, "I feel that ..." Of course, whatever you say after the word "that" is an opinion, not a feeling. Many are confused about the difference between giving opinions and sharing how they are feeling, and yet it is the feeling that reveals the person. Two people watching the same sunset side by side can be feeling totally different things. One might be filled with joy and wonder because of God's beautiful creation while the other might be filled with sadness and loss, thinking that the last time they saw a sunset like this was with a loved one who has since passed away. Most would assume that they were feeling the same and miss a beautiful opportunity for intimacy by not sharing their feelings. The feelings tell us who the person is at that moment.

Our experience preparing for a recent trip that we took is another great example of this. On the surface, we were both excited as we planned and both anticipated going. We had discussed the finances and made arrangements for an empty house, but when it came to going to the airport, we discovered that one of us (and no, we're not going to tell you who) had some underlying feelings of insecurity, anxiety, and even fear about leaving the kids and unfinished business, which caused a delay in packing. The other of us discovered that it was definitely not good for the relationship to sit in the car and honk the horn. When we got in touch with the feelings, we could readily see how we needed to be compassionate and supportive toward each other.

"So many times miracles have happened in our couple relationship or our family when we are able to share difficult or negative feelings. Sometimes when I share negative feelings, it's just to be heard; other times it actually leads to resolving conflicts. It's a miracle when sharing what seems so negative leads to forgiveness or even healing and forgetting. One example of this occurred at a family meeting when Chrysy shared how disgusted she

felt to constantly have to deal with Danny's hair on the bar of soap. Danny didn't have a clue. It was so beautiful the way Danny's empathy for Chrysy's feelings allowed him to make changes for her. The sharing situation is so crucial because if the same things were said outside of sharing, they would come across as pure and simple criticism. When we're sharing, however, we are open to listening." —Betty

Often we allow our feelings to control our behaviors, and by taking the time to dialogue or look introspectively at them, we can resolve so many different areas of needless conflict. These feelings can ruin us and can escalate into hatred if not shared. It's a simple solution, but it takes effort to create a safe time and place. Too often, we don't take the time to express our negative feelings but rather sweep them under the rug to fester and ruin an otherwise wonderful relationship. You, your spouse, and your children have to be able to openly discuss the way you feel in a sharing environment (one without judgment or criticism). After we let others know us and hopefully understand us, we can move on to forgiveness and healing.

"Sometimes I'm afraid to tell Betty how I really feel. I want her to think that I'm strong and want to reassure her that everything is okay. I try to hide that I'm feeling insecure or defeated, feeling like a failure. I pretend that I'm calm and have everything under control to keep her from worrying. I'm afraid that by sharing what's really going on inside me, she would lose heart, too, or lose faith in me. But when I do share honestly, she is compassionate, caring, and even more loving. She feels needed and wanted and tries to support me even more. She showers me with love because I am vulnerable with her and she knows that she can trust me. Sharing the difficult feelings builds true intimacy because I know that she loves the real me and not the facade. I feel so loved and appreciated and warm and supported. After sharing a feeling like this and being accepted by Betty, I feel a warm glow of closeness and intimacy." —Ed

Sticks and Stones

Whoever made up that old saying, "Sticks and stones may break my bones, but words will never hurt me," was a moron. Words do hurt, but it helps to understand the cause behind them. Harsh words are often the result of unexpressed feelings. When we think of this, so many things come to mind: kids saying, "I hate you," or "You are the worst parent in the world," swear words, backtalk, disrespect, and yelling and fighting even with other siblings. In all of these cases, if you were to listen to the words, it would drive you crazy. It is so important to realize how little training we have in expressing real feelings. Our society is so confused because so many people express their opinions as feelings, but everyone, young and old alike, reacts to their feelings whether they want to or not.

We are not trained to look inside and recognize when we are hurt, embarrassed, lonely, empty, angry, happy, or sad. If we were trained, we would realize that we are often choosing words to get attention or revenge or to fight back as a reaction to what we are feeling. One of our biggest improvements as parents happened when a kid said, "I hate you." To be able to hold back a reaction and simply say, "You must be feeling really hurt or angry right now," was a huge growth step for us. Nine times out of ten, that would almost end it. The child got that we knew how he or she was feeling, and the confrontation would not escalate into a huge conflict. Often, within a short time, we could get to the root of the issue and come up with a solution.

It is best for mature adults to ignore the words and behaviors that they don't like and tune into the young ones' feelings. It takes so much understanding and effort trying to remember what it was like to be a child. Children don't have all of the experiences and lessons of the adult. They are dealing with their own limited knowledge. They may say many things that they don't mean. The bottom line is that one needs to ignore the bad and praise the good. It is important to verbalize feelings for children regardless of age, because they may not be connecting how they are feeling with how they are behaving or talking. So many instances come to mind with regard to verbalizing feelings, especially for small kids.

"Once when we were at church with our grandchildren, Skylor was upset with Taylor and was hiding her head in her hands. I asked if she was feeling angry and if I could hold her up to show her what was happening. She immediately snapped out of it. It is so important to try to guess how children might be feeling. If you guess right and express to them what they are feeling, it gives them great reassurance. They know that someone understands them and that they are not alone. When time and the situation permit, I think it is important to even ask them where their feeling is in their body and help them get to know it even better." —Ed

Is it in your stomach like a knot? Is it tightness in your chest? Do you feel sad and heavy in your shoulders? Actually pinpointing the feeling is great for helping kids to really start to connect feelings with what's going on in their body. The more you show little ones that you understand what is going on inside, the better. It's hard though, because it is so normal just to say, "Stop acting like that." We focus only on the behavior instead of recognizing that feelings are behind the behavior. Just a little conscious effort can go miles in getting the behavior that you want. Feelings not spoken out are acted out. You have to speak out the feelings for kids.

Does This Purse Go with My Shoes?

Why is it that we are more concerned with matching our clothes than with matching our feelings to our past experiences? When a couple or family has certain feelings simultaneously, recalling that experience can be a triggering device to feel it again. The deepest form of listening is when two or more people experience the same feeling at the same time. Often, it is accompanied by knowing glances and gestures, the need to hold hands or hug, and the general feeling of intimacy and unity. It is also one of the quickest ways to get the other person to relate to how you are currently feeling. And it's amazing how a memory of a past experience will often pop into your head when you're trying to describe a current feeling that is similar—for instance, it is the type of excitement that we felt going to the Sugar Bowl game or the kind of excitement and joy after the birth of a child. These are really two different feelings of excitement, but relating the mutual experience really starts to bring it to life for the other person.

"For me, matching feelings to past experiences is the most graphic way to describe feelings. If it's a feeling that you have personally had before, then it fully brings it to life inside you once again. Then, you can describe better what's going on inside you at that very moment. If I try to imagine what the other person had going on, I might say, 'I believe this is a feeling you had kicking the winning goal.' This demonstrates great giving and caring. If I can recall a mutual experience, I might say, 'I believe we had this feeling when we were in this situation together,' then it brings the greatest empathy and closeness of all. For instance, 'It's the awe and exuberance we had when we found out that Baby Danny's jaundice count was down.' We knew that we had experienced a miracle." —Betty

The family that shares humor and feelings not only stays together, but experiences rich moments of joy and closeness. Life is a journey, and learning new things to make it better should not be all work and no play. Life is too short to be serious all the time. Humor is a powerful tool, especially when shared with those we love, so please have a laugh on us. Try to remember the last hilarious joke you heard or funny family video you saw, and just have fun with it.

Chapter 4
Feelings and Humor

Passionate Points

Humor and laughter are life saving and absolutely necessary in parenting. Start now to write down and frequently relive and share comical family experiences. Find your favorite family movies, shows, or books that have lines that "speak to you".

Feelings not spoken out are acted out! Our moods, attitudes, level of participation, and many decisions are controlled by our feelings. Yet most of us don't take the time to look inside to see this powerful driving force behind our behaviors. We just act and react to life.

Verbalize feelings for children. Instead of constantly correcting behaviors imagine the feeling behind the behavior and point that out first. For instance, as you gently pull your toddler away say, "You must be feeling very angry or hurt right now, but it's not okay to hit other people".

Dialogue Questions

What are two of the most comical experiences we have had as a couple or family? How do I feel sharing these with you now?

What feeling do I find most difficult to share with you right now? Describe it in loving detail.

Family Meeting Sharing Questions

(Go around the family circle again and again) Share a family memory that makes you smile or laugh?

What upsets, frustrates or bugs me the most in our family right now? How does it make me feel sharing this with all of you?

Chapter 5

Consequences: Logical and Natural

Never raise your hands to your kids.
It leaves your groin unprotected.

—Red Buttons

As humans, we all need structure in our lives. We all have our routines, which we learn to actually appreciate. We even get frustrated when things don't go our way (e.g., if there is too much traffic, if we have to stop at too many red lights, if lines are too long). As much as you want to put the pedal to the metal and crash into the car in front of you in which the lady is gabbing on her cell and making you miss the light, you know there are consequences. When we get up each morning, we might look forward to the freshly brewed cup of coffee before we start our day. If we walk into the kitchen and the coffee pot is broken, or if we have to wait in a long line at the coffee shop, there is interference in our routine. As a result, we might feel irritated, uneasy, or even a little overwhelmed—or, if we're truly addicted to caffeine, turn into the Incredible Hulk.

It is no surprise that structure is important for effective parenting. Children thrive on routines.

They depend on those things even if they appear as though they do not care for them at times. If children know that there are clearly defined rules and limits, that is half of the battle. Children, in turn, must also know that there are equally clear and defined logical consequences for their actions, and parents must be ready to live with the consequences as well. Routines and schedules help provide a sense of stability for the entire family. If, for example, a child knows when he is expected to go to bed, a toddler knows that hitting is not allowed, and a teen knows when curfew is, then you have clearly defined your expectation of them. If the child still chooses to break the rule or expectation, then the parent is not the bad guy; rather, enforcing the consequence enhances respect for the parent. Stability is vital to any family and allows children to feel secure, safe, cared for, and empowered by their parents. This provides a better atmosphere for the entire family unit.

Parents should have open communication with their children. Often, the family needs to sit down and talk about rules, consequences, and routines. Children who have a voice in the family feel more valued as a person. Parents who show greater understanding and respond to their children's needs and problems will earn more respect than the parent who demands it. Parents who allow the entire family to make decisions collaboratively will see their children learn to evaluate things better, learn how to make decisions in school, and learn to trust more fully, because they are a part of the overall process.

While responsibility for the safety and well-being of the child rests with the parent, it is important for the children to know that they count and that their thoughts and feelings are taken seriously. As children get older, it is important to have them establish their own consequences with as much feedback and guidance as they need, so that the final decision does not always have to lie with the parents. While the parents are still the ones ultimately in charge, they need to communicate, that when they have to make the final decision, it will be based on input from the whole family plus what is most reasonable, safe, and logical. This establishes cohesion and provides the opportunity for teamwork, which results in open communication.

There are numerous types of parenting styles used in our world. Everyone has his or her own opinion as to what works best. However, simply earning respect from children, having an open form of communication, and instilling morals and values are all important no matter which type of parenting style is used. A balanced parenting style with clear expectations, defined limits, consequences, and fairness is very effective. It not only teaches vital skills to the children, but models the behaviors that will make them become successful parents as well. This type of parenting shows that the parents are involved in their children's lives, understand their concerns, are flexible, and are in charge without having to be authoritarian. There are structures, limits, rules, boundaries, consequences, and positive reinforcement. Children with this kind of parenting tend to do well socially in life. They tend to get along with others while reacting to things in a positive way. This kind of parenting produces balanced, contented, and happy children. Proper discipline strategies aid children in their everyday lives and teach them to become responsible adults with self-discipline and consideration for other people.

"In my Sarano Kelley coaching program, I have had to establish consequences for failing to accomplish any of my daily activities. This has confirmed their power and effectiveness for keeping me on track. In the past, we used self-imposed, logical consequences in order to stop swearing. We put money in a bucket every time we slipped or got caught. Of the two types of consequences, natural and logical, I found that being aware and allowing natural consequences to run their course was hard at first, but became easier with practice. For instance after turning the duty of laundry over to the kids, the natural consequence was that, if they didn't wash their clothes, at some point they would have to wear dirty clothes! The hardest part of that was to not feel like the dirty shirt was a reflection on us as parents and homemakers. On the other hand, the difficult part of logical consequences is that they require preplanning and clarity. But once established, they allow the complete transfer of responsibility to the child without punishment or negativity. The most important thing is to follow up with consequences once agreed upon."
—Ed

If parents use consequences with clearly defined limits, model by example, and show positive communication, they will encourage good behavior in their children. This will help to keep the lines of communication open between the parent and child. It will promote honesty that will carry over to other parts of their lives as well. Parents who affirm the positive actions of their children help them gain self-confidence. Focusing on the good behaviors and praising children for these actions will help them have positive behaviors at school and with friends. Keep in mind that consequences are there to discuss boundaries and reinforce rules in a positive way. If a parent uses consequences that do not fit the action, the consequences will be ineffective for teaching boundaries to the children.

Life is dynamic and ever-changing, and children grow, mature, and change as well. The same consequence that works today may not work even two weeks from now. Like everything else, consequences and guidelines need to be reestablished whenever they become ineffective. One caution is to remember that we as parents also have to be willing to live with the child's choice. For instance, if a consequence for not doing homework is that the child can't go to a friend's party, we may assume that the child would not want to miss it for the world. We enjoy being with the friend's parents and make arrangements to help them with the food and entertainment. The day before the party, we find out that our child did not do the homework. How do you live with the child's choice now? Be careful when you set up logical consequences and avoid those that make it difficult to follow through. We laugh now when we think of how we used to say things like, "If you don't do your homework, I'm going to kill you!"

If You Touch the Stove, You're Going to Burn Your Finger

Facing consequences is a part of growing up. We all have dealt with natural consequences in our lives. As adults, if we do not go to work, we will not have a job. If we do not pay our bills, we will lose the house, car, or other possessions. If we speed, we will eventually get caught and get a ticket. Children are also faced with natural consequences. During these learning times, our children are taught lessons without the parents' intervention. Some of these lessons can be positive learning experiences while others can be dangerous. If children do not complete their homework, the teacher will give them a zero. If they do not follow safety rules, such as watching for cars before they cross the street, the result can be injury or even death.

Parents need to intervene when we know that something could cause serious injury, and we must verbalize the consequence without allowing it to happen. There are other times when the consequence is not that serious, such as when the child doesn't make a lunch and goes hungry, or is roughhousing with a sibling until one gets hurt; in such cases, we can sit quietly and watch. After a child experiences one of these consequences, it is good to run through it to teach how to think through the situation before it happens. For instance, "Tony, next time you are tempted to watch TV instead of doing your homework, you should imagine the next day at school and what it will feel like when the teacher calls on you and you have to say in front of the class that you did not do it. Then imagine having to sit through detention after school while all of your friends are out playing, and finally imagine what happens when you have to bring the note from the teacher home to us and how you feel when you have to get us to sign it."

As parents, we hope and pray that our children are thinking through these things all of the time. The reality is that they are not. Growing up is hard, and learning these lessons the natural way is a part of it. Other examples that children face are refusing to stop climbing on furniture, then falling on the ground; being told that the oven is hot, then touching it and getting burned; and being told that the food is spicy, then taking a bite and having a burned mouth. It is our job to protect our children from harm, but we won't be there all the time to make sure that the consequence does not get out of hand. Unfortunately, the end result is that many behaviors may lead to injury. For example, through peer pressure a teenager might persuade a friend to take drugs. He or she might even do it in front of the friend to prove there will be no harm. The other person might try it just once and be seriously injured or even die from the drug. Parents are constantly worried for their children's safety and for all of these natural consequences in their lives. Although we all have to learn and grow, this type of consequence sure makes our hearts jump thinking of the possible outcomes to our precious babies. That is why it is so important to instill the skill of thinking through in advance what might happen.

"I watched and listened and noticed last night while Chrysy was attempting to get her daughter Taylor to bed. It took me right back to when I was in the same situation. Now I could see that without clear consequences, I would get

frustrated and start punishing to handle the situation. How much better to give Taylor a sticker on a chart with a goal of getting 5 nights in a row for an ice cream cone. If she doesn't get to bed on time, the consequence is that she must start over again. Setting consequences up ahead of time is so peace-promoting. Natural consequences are my favorite and are the best teachers, but logical ones are also important with perfect planning. They all keep the parent sane and unfrustrated. Love it." —Betty

Logical consequences are an important discipline strategy. If a child makes a mess, he or she would be expected to clean it up. If they have a fit in the middle of the grocery store, they might get a toy taken away when they get home. If they are out past their curfew, they might be grounded. If they make a bad grade in school, they may be required to have tutoring and lose television privileges. This kind of discipline strategy gets the children thinking about what they have done and the result of their actions. Although it should be difficult or uncomfortable for the child to take the punishment, he or she understands that it was his or her own action and choice. It ultimately goes back to the responsibility of the child, who is the owner of the decision.

"Betty and I had long since learned that force never works with a strong-willed child. At a parent conference, we were told that Kellie had not achieved high enough grades to advance to the eighth grade and that she was given an alternative to have a tutor for the summer to get caught up. At that moment, we knew that the best thing we could do was to allow her to make her own decision as to whether or not she wanted to repeat the seventh grade. So we simply said, 'Kellie, if you want to repeat seventh grade, we will be there for you, and we'll spend the summer like we always do. If you want to take a tutor, we will help support you by paying for that tutor. Even though it's very expensive, we will do that for you. But, you have to tell us what you want to do. We're here to love and support you either way.' Kellie proceeded to choose the tutor. In the eighth grade, she became the student body president, got straight A's throughout the school year, blossomed, was totally into all of the activities at school, and simply became a minor miracle. Of course, we owe that to unconditional love and unconditional parenting, trusting that if we were really willing to give her full responsibility, she would make the best choice for herself. Thank goodness she did, but even if she had not, it would

not have been the end of the world. It was a tremendous growth time for both us as parents as well as for her." —Ed

The two attitudes that parents must have in order to make consequences work are clarity and positiveness. Clarity means knowing exactly what your expectations are and when your child has or has not met them. Positiveness means to actually delight when your child tests the limits by experiencing the reality of challenging a consequence. As children accomplish important milestones, complete chores, or learn from mistakes, it is vital that each parent recognize this and take that moment to give positive feedback to the child. Parents also need to check from time to time to make sure they are not sending mixed messages to children. There is no perfect adult; therefore, we cannot expect there to be a perfect child. All children will make mistakes and show negative behaviors. Dealing with these behaviors positively as a parent can make all the difference in maintaining the close bond with the child. Parents need to show consistency with any consequence while keeping the communication open. Many learning opportunities for both adult and child show up every day.

"Taking the anger out of parenting is a big one for me because I was a very angry parent for years. I had some attitudes like, 'I deserve respect because I am the parent', or 'Whatever it is that the kids are doing is directed at me personally.' Another one was that if they did something in front of others, it was a direct reflection on me as a parent. But during all that time, I was really not clear about what I wanted from the kids. I would accept a certain behavior as okay when it didn't bother me, but then the same behavior could upset me and irritate me at other times. I would want instant results sometimes, but then I'd let them get away with murder at other times. I was just a confused, mixed-message parent who got exactly what he put out: confused, mixed-message behavior. I truly regret those times that we spanked. I know that we never injured the children, but I always had a sick feeling in my gut afterward. It was as though I was incapable of handling things without being the bully. I know that spanking is just not necessary any more as a parent, and I'm so thankful that we found ways to deal with our own frustration and learned to discipline without anger." —Ed

Setting Them Up for Success

As parents, one of our goals is to teach personal responsibility, which builds self-esteem and self-pride. These characteristics are necessary in order for a child to become a productive member of society. At times, it is a difficult job being parents. It is easy to get wrapped up in everything that your children do wrong rather than focus on what they do right. Any child needs boundaries and consequences for his behavior. You will only do your children more harm than good in the long term if you just let them get away with everything they do. A disciplined structure teaches them responsibility and helps them gain self-esteem and pride in a positive manner. It is good for all children to have chores around the house. As long as they are chores that the child is quite capable of doing, it will actually build up self-esteem when complete and will give a sense of pride in doing them perfectly. A reward system, which works well for doing chores and making them fun, encourages your child to make them a habit. We had elaborate chore charts that gave each child a variety of tasks that could be easily accomplished. More difficult jobs required the pairing up of two people, and more distasteful jobs like cleaning the toilet didn't come around too often. Sometimes the rewards were immediate and small, like a few M&M's, or a sticker, or sometimes they came at the end of a successful week, like a movie or sporting event.

Always encourage your child to do his best and give him lots of praise when he tries new things so that he can reach his full potential. Then remember to sit back and enjoy the fruits of your labor. The blessing of having had children is one of those experiences that will continuously have an impact on your journey through life. By instilling pride, self-esteem, and responsibility in your children, you not only accomplish something essential, but you will truly enjoy it as well.

Although our primary focus was setting an example through our own actions, we spent quality time, especially at the dinner table, sharing stories of our own childhood. We shared comical, hurtful, dangerous, and regretful experiences. This activity had a dual effect. It let the kids know that they could share their experiences with us and we would understand. Also, it taught them lessons that they wouldn't have to try for themselves.

All of this communication played a vital role in our daily interactions. It gave us a chance to have input into what they were hearing and seeing as well as the opportunity to send messages in ways that they could understand and accept. Children need adults to guide them in choosing the right words to express themselves. Teaching by example is the most effective tool for parents.

The Proverbial Line in the Sand

Every sibling who has ever had to share a room has, at some point, gotten into a fight and divided their room with a long stretch of tape. The problem is that usually one poor sap gets stuck using the window as a door. As parents, it is our job to maintain order in the household in a collaborative way. The whole goal of setting logical consequences is to be able to parent without emotion and in a nonpunitive way. It requires setting up the consequence with the children long before the problem happens, The best way we know to do this is in family meetings, and it is always important to involve all of the children in the decision-making process. The first part of this job is to set clearly defined limits with our children. They need to know how to act, react, and behave, as well as understand exactly what is expected of them. In addition to providing safety and order to the family, these limits can be used to teach them the difference between right and wrong, good and bad. This helps them inside the household, with peers, and in school as well.

The best way to keep everyday behavior good is to "nip it in the bud". Correcting the problem when it is small prevents it from escalating. The system of "point outs" was a way for us to avoid power struggles and keep anger and frustration out of our parenting. This system is easily setup through family meetings. First, you would come to an agreement with the children to use this method instead of yelling, controlling, force, or whatever is not enjoyable for the parent or child now. Everyone agreed that they wanted the environment of our home to be a refuge and a sanctuary of peace and happiness. A "point out" was a reminder that whatever was going on was not in keeping with this ideal. The concept of "point outs" runs in time blocks, so for instance, you might say, during the next hour, three point outs will lead to a time out. For that hour as you go about your daily life, if a child gets whiney, or begins to pick a fight with a sibling or you feel irritated, simply say, "point out". The child has agreed to run and touch a designated spot, like a door knob, and come back. It is amazing how this break in the action gives everyone a chance to refresh, diffuse feelings and start over again. No raised voice and no animosity to it. If the child gets three "point outs" during that time period, they then have a time out in their bedroom. The length is based on age with one minute for one year olds, two for two year olds, etc. This system puts the power in the children to decide whether to cooperate or put themselves in time out. The parent is not the bad guy.

Children who know their boundaries usually demonstrate positive behaviors and live far away from the limits. With these clearly defined expectations, there is no gray area should the child decide to cross the line. Actually, it is good for children to test the limits at times, and we as parents should not be disappointed or upset when they do. That is why we went through all the trouble of setting up the limit and consequence in the first place. We readily oblige their test by helping the child enforce the consequence and move on.

There will be times when we have not thought of a particular consequence in advance. These unexpected things happen all the time, like a child breaking a toy in a store or taking someone else's things while visiting a friend's house. We correct the situation immediately and make certain that the child understands the misbehavior. Next, we take time with this child to decide what the consequence will be if this situation ever arises again. Sometimes misbehavior is so blatant that it must be handled with a consequence right away. At these times, we sit down with the culprit, and each (child and parent) give input on a consequence. We have often found that the child's consequence was more extreme than ours, but we usually chose an adjusted version of the child's choice of discipline. If we couldn't agree, our consequence would be firm and fair, and we made sure that the child could understand the reason behind it.

"I was always told and taught that everything our children did was because we were or were not excellent parents. It was my parents talking. That

brought a tremendous amount of pressure and stress to our lives. What a relief to find out that this wasn't totally true. We learned parenting skills, carried them out to our best ability, and prayed for the rest. We often heard the saying that great parents can have lousy kids and lousy parents can have great kids. We didn't want to leave it to chance so we did everything humanly possible to achieve greatness. What is great? Children who are responsible, cooperative, happy, and loving people" —Betty

It is important to make limits clear and realistic to the child. Think of limits as expectations for positive behavior. It is important that parents set expectations that they know are appropriate based on the age and maturity of the children. This shows the children that you have faith in their ability to follow the rules. If a parent sets impossible expectations, the children will be disappointed, as will the adult. Setting reasonable limits can show children how good it feels to do the right thing and follow the rules. Our entire society is structured with laws, rules, and regulations, and the working world has clearly defined limits and expectations for behavior. As parents, this is only one of the many steps that we will take to ensure that our children become mature, responsible, and productive adults.

"For too long I gave the kids total control over my hot buttons. They knew exactly how angry I would get if they did stuff—especially in front of our friends or others in public. They could probably see the terror in my body. I think it is a lot like taking the dogs out when another dog comes into sight, already knowing that they're going to bark and charge. For years I assumed that everyone was judging us based on our kids. I always became hyper when we went to restaurants or other occasions where certain standards of behavior and etiquette were expected. It's like I almost knew in advance that stuff would happen. It was such a relief when we discovered later how to play games or act like the restaurant was our house and not get hung up on perfect behavior but truly enjoy being with the kids. I still laugh when I think of the doorbell sound at Yum Yum Tree, where we would say, 'make sure the butler gets the door; it sounds like another guest is arriving,' and when we would pretend the 'maid' delivered food to our table. I truly get excited and feel so relieved when I think of turning those same occasions that used to be nightmares into joyful, happy times." —Ed

Children who have clearly defined limits will understand the world better, learn how to interact with others, and have better self-esteem. They will tend to stay in school, keep jobs, and develop healthy relationships with others. The love that we have for our children is so strong. We are obligated as parents to provide guidance, patience, expectations, and consequences.

Stop It Mom; You're Embarrassing Me

Research has proven that the impact of touch and affection with infants is vital to the social aspects they will exhibit in the future. Babies who are left in cribs without the feeling of skin, touch, or cuddling often cry, are unsatisfied, and later exhibit social problems. A mother who delivers a new baby is strongly encouraged to hold the infant immediately to form that instant bond. Women who choose to breastfeed form closeness with that baby, and the bonding time is special and unique only to those two individuals.

"I learned the value of nurturing and showing affection from one of the first books I read when I was pregnant with Jenny: Ashley Montegue's Touching. *Hugs, touching, back rubs, massages, scratching the back, gentleness, caressing, holding hands, sitting side by side, are all ways to do this. These signs of affection must be done by both mother and father. This actually teaches fathers and husbands how to be more affectionate to their wives, also. When is affection appropriate? We have found that kids will reject affection if they believe it is not appropriate. This will definitely happen when their friends are around! But whenever you are alone together, and often throughout the day, find those special moments to show your love— especially when waking the kids up or putting them to sleep, and when getting back together after a separation in the day. Each child (both boys and girls) deserves the same nurturing and affection. There should be no discrimination. Sometimes girls can be treated more gently, and sometimes it means dog piles for boys, but touching is always vital."* —Betty

We must not underestimate the power of affection in the family. Now, we don't want to love on them like Lenny loves the rabbit in *Of Mice and Men*, but we do want to show them as much affection as possible. Love thrives in and through affection. We hope that when we show love and affection to our spouses and children, they will feel free to demonstrate this as well. The parent-child relationship is improved because of the positive emotions and happiness that this nurturing provides. Babies begin life needing cuddles, hugs, kisses, and special bonding times that help develop security and trust. They then feel loved, cared for, and safe. As children grow older, they still need and appreciate the strong affection given by parents that helps them learn to be more loving and trusting to others.

"I realize how important it was for me to be physically close to our children. I know that I did not feel enough of that at times from my own father, so I really wanted our children to experience the hugs and love of a father. With the boys, a lot of contact came during games, but as the girls grew older, I started to allow so many taboos in our society to limit the contact. It was very important to learn that it is the father who confirms the sexuality of the girls around the age of puberty. So I made it a point to be aware and to frequently tell them how beautiful they were, to be there for them, to hug when they were upset, and be available to listen. I will preserve forever in my heart the times of holding a sobbing teen with a broken heart or hearing those special words, 'You and me, Daddy.' One of my favorites was to wake them by flopping into bed to give the children a triple hug with Betty. With the younger kids, as soon as they could understand, I would cuddle every night with them to say night prayers. I always asked God to hold them in His arms and to love them as much as I did. These times are so precious and warm and delightful." —Ed

Chapter 5
Consequences: Logical and Natural

Passionate Points

Natural Consequences happen because of the laws of nature, but logical consequences require planning, agreements and regular modification. They are most effective when decided upon in collaboration with the whole family.

Catch your kids doing something right with more excitement and energy than you use when you are catching them doing something wrong. Focus on praising the good and ignoring the bad.

The sure sign that something is wrong is when you don't have to make changes. As long as you and your children are growing, change is normal.

Dialogue Questions

What can I do to make sure I follow through on consequences? How do I feel about that?

What is the biggest point of conflict between us and our children right now? What change can we make in our system of discipline to better handle it? How do I feel sharing this with you?

Family Meeting Sharing Questions

For our home to be a refuge, what are the agreements we need to implement and are willing to follow?

What is the consequence for each of these broken agreements?

Chapter 6

Playing Together and Family Days

I've got seven kids. The three words you hear most around my house are "hello," "goodbye," and "I'm pregnant."

—Dean Martin

Wow! Children grow so fast! The time we have with them is so precious. We want to cherish each and every day because we can't get those moments back. One of the ways to spend quality time together is to learn how to develop connections with each other that will last a lifetime. As we all know, establishing relationships is an important part of life. We need to have positive working relationships with coworkers; we need to have good relationships with our neighbors. Lasting friendships are a result of people building close bonds when together and are sustained even if separated by time and distance. Every time you meet again, you pick up right where you left off. Therefore, it should not be a surprise that we need to work on the relationships in our own home as well, since it is the training ground for life. This work takes love, patience, dedication, and positive communication. Spending precious time together as a family can help support and maintain those bonds. It is also the best way to envision dreams, set goals, and enjoy each other's company. That's why Family Days became so important to us and were the core and the foundation of our close family.

For us, Family Days were an awesome day once a week (usually Sunday) that had a packed agenda with a prayerful spiritual beginning, followed by a one-hour family meeting, and then a variety of activities. They included an excursion, games, a tailgate party for a football game on TV, or many other things that just felt like mini-vacations. All homework for the kids had to be completed before this day and no work for the adults could interfere. It was sacred time set aside for all of us to soak up each other's company. Family Day was an item in our budget, and enough money was set aside to make it exciting. Some days would cost less, and each month we could save up for days that were more expensive. This commitment of time and attention and money gave us so many opportunities to bond and grow closer.

Peaceful and healthy relationships are an important part of human life, but they're not always a part of family life (especially if you're in a 900-square-foot home—which we lived in for several years—with eight people!). The closer and more vulnerable you are, the easier it is to hurt and be hurt. And believe us, we were close in that small house. Thriving permanent relationships in our families don't happen by accident. They take constant attention and require the consideration of several factors. Intimate closeness grows as long as everyone thinks of others before themselves. When disagreements or philosophical differences occur, learn to agree to disagree and live in harmony. The parents lead the family by example. Whatever they make real by practicing with each other, like no swearing or yelling, will be passed on to their children. It takes time and energy for the two to decide what's really important, to work these things out in their own life, and to incorporate them into the family life. Another factor is how things change as the children grow. Whether it's infants to toddlers or preteens to teenagers, the interactions and skills have to be adapted to these variances no matter what age the children are or how many years there are between each child. Family life doesn't stop when the children are grown, but rather turns into somewhat of a friendship/mentor phase. The grown children feel comfortable asking for, and actually appreciate, input and ideas in all areas of their lives, including raising their own children. Intimacy flourishes when the family chooses to share feelings openly, to help each other through difficult times, and to love one another no matter what.

"When we gather as a family, so many positive things can happen. We are so powerful together. One activity that we did every year at a family meeting was to set goals in various areas, like physical, school or business-related, spiritual, hobbies/sports, and family communication and activities. Before we would set these goals, we would look at last year's goals and see how we had done. It was so encouraging to see our accomplishments as we moved on to improve ourselves. Another activity was to dream together. One time we sat in the living room of our very small home and dreamed big dreams on butcher paper. We still have that paper. We dreamed about each child having his or her own bedroom—a space to go to and decorate just the way he or she wanted. We dreamed about going to Disneyland and about other wonderful adventures. These dreams came true." —Betty

The sharing time in family meetings is when you get to know each other, and it will do more to build closeness than all of the games, chores, or activities that you can do together. It's the foundation upon which trust, respect, caring, and cooperation are built. Especially when there are disagreements, sharing gives you an opportunity to get to know what it really means to each of you. Then it is possible to have empathy and understand the perspective of each other. We could spend all day doing a project with bickering, hassles, fights, and confrontation and not finish. But there were times when we would spend most of the time sharing and then the project seemed to get done in no time. There are very strict rules for sharing in family meetings. (1) Everyone gets a chance to share, but it is okay to pass when it is your turn. Sharing can be directed by a question like, "What do you like most about the person sitting to your left?" But it can be non-directed, in which case everyone is encouraged to share anything that is important to them at that moment—either positive or negative. (2) Anything shared is held in confidence. (3) While someone is sharing, there are no comments or interruptions. The only response allowed is clarification, for instance, "Did I hear you say ...?" or "Are you finished?" (4) If there are issues or misunderstandings that come up as a result of the sharing, they would be resolved by the parties involved outside of sharing time. The caring and cooperation that flows from these times together foster the trust and respect for each other that carry over not only to the rest of our meeting but to the rest of our lives.

"Family meetings are the cornerstone upon which everything else that we do in a family is based. Without family meetings, we are just like other families that we see around us. We notice that we turn into people with personal hidden agendas, which results in bickering, fragmentation, and even kids conspiring against parents. With family meetings, we are a fine, well-oiled machine! It is so amazing how putting the relationship over activity is like putting the icing on the cake of activities. Everything is smooth, creamy, and efficient when we feel unified and connected first. When big projects need to get done, lots of people would think that sitting around and sharing would be a waste of time. They feel the need to just be doing. Having that attitude will result in a waste of time. Relationship first and 'business' second is the only way to go." —Ed

R-E-S-P-E-C-T, Find Out What It Means to Me
Don't Sock Your Brother; Don't Sock Your Sister

Many believe that we must first respect ourselves before we can respect others, which falls under the huge category of belief that you can't give away what you don't have. The first thing is to make sure that you have a healthy respect for yourself, including your own body. Some people get hung up thinking that spiritual is good but body is bad. We need to instill in our family constantly that both of these are what God created and both are good. This leads to respecting our bodies by developing healthy habits and staying away from the misuse of drugs, sexual behaviors, and destructive tendencies.

Respecting our children teaches and guides them to respect others not only in the family, but also in school, personal friendships, and later in their jobs. Showing our kids respect raises their self-esteem because they believe that they are valued as individuals. Listening to their thoughts, concerns, and feelings shows them that a parent cares. As a result, children will be much more independent and strong because they will know that they matter.

When there are different opinions in any family, it is important to work things out through listening and communicating what it means to you. We share openly and listen intently so that we really know the person behind the thoughts, opinions, and ideas. This allows us to respect each other with empathy and accept the person even when we disagree. Difference of opinion is what this world is made of, but knowing how to deal with disagreements makes all the difference in the world. It is essential to allow children to have their opinions in order to build their self-esteem. Parents must be prepared to turn it into a teachable moment if those opinions could harm themselves, their future, or someone else, and must guide them in a way that shows respect.

Teaching cooperation and coping skills also enhances respect and trust, which are key for building a stronger family unit. Sometimes children do not cooperate because they need some attention. They might need to be heard about something, might have a problem at school, or even might have a strong and legitimate thought about the cause of their noncooperation. This is a huge opportunity for a parent to take the time to do some active listening. Sit down with the one who needs attention. Maybe even hold hands. Look him or her in the eyes and give the child the space to talk while asking, "Is there anything else you'd like to say?" Continue asking until the child truly feels like he or she has been heard and accepted. If things come up that need to be corrected or adjusted, make note of it to bring up later and perhaps say that it will be discussed soon. But for right then in that precious moment, be sure that the child truly feels heard, respected, and loved. Listening is loving. When the child feels listened to in this complete way, he or she feels truly and fully loved.

Parents can teach cooperation by having their children help with household chores, meeting to discuss plans, and even brainstorming about upcoming family events. Whenever parents see children helping one another and cooperating in a positive way, they should recognize this desirable behavior with words of praise and affirmation. Including the children in decision making will allow them to feel important, and when they come up with a good idea, let them know it. Simply asking their input and ideas will make them feel valued, and they will find it easier to get along with one another. Kids demonstrate tremendous cooperation when time is spent setting up rules and guidelines together because they feel a stake in them. It makes sense and seems fair. They are definitely more likely to stick to decisions when they have had a say in making them.

"What are the possibilities for family meetings? Of course, the list is endless. Topics can be everything from goals for next year to 'How do you feel about Kellie's new boyfriend'? We run the gamut. The most important thing is to provide a safe way for people to express their position, judgment, feelings, opinions, and beliefs. The trick is to make everyone feel listened to and to do so in an environment where they can do this without interruption. Sometimes, there is anger, hurt, and tears, and sometimes—like when we share the best quality of the person to our right—there is laughter and joy. Over and over we have experienced the miracle of peace, harmony, and joy that flows forth when people are allowed to be real and share from the heart. I think the key is setting the guidelines for sharing without trying to force things. Don't require that people be involved and share, but just let them experience what is going on. Eventually the trust and intimacy will allow everyone to feel safe to be open. We had no idea how far we had come until we got the perspective of an outsider. I think of the first few meetings after a fiancé or a spouse joined us for the first time. Usually they were amazed and blown away by how everyone could share anything they wanted. It was very difficult to be brought into a situation at that level, especially if they had never experienced anything like it before. It wasn't long before this environment allowed them to blend in and start suggesting topics they wished to explore." —Ed

There is really no age limit for when to start having family meetings. The sooner children get used to them the better. Even toddlers could sit on our laps and feel connected and involved. Lines of communication are kept open and prove to be beneficial when a child is going through rough times or great times and is just bursting to share. As a result, children develop coping skills because they know they have a foundation of support. Also, they learn that some things in life take negotiation and a sense of give and take. Family meetings do need to be regular and have a separate special time away from mealtimes. In any event, regularly scheduled, structured meetings keep the relationships running smoothly and avoid the big blowups. Some families have a meeting once a week, some once a month. This strategy allows everyone to participate in the decision-making process. Meetings could include simple things like planning a weekly menu or upcoming event. They might be spiritual in which the family meets for some special time honoring God, praying together, reading the Bible, and applying the lessons to everyday life. Meetings can also be a time to discuss tough issues like drugs, alcohol, and peer pressure.

Load Up the Station Wagon

There are so many fun activities that families can do together. In addition to committed family days, you can have game nights, shopping days, fun skits, campouts (even in your own backyard), chore day, and even just family relax time. Any of these can be made fun, create lasting memories, build closeness, and teach children planning and cooperation skills. Whenever possible, a family meeting should be included.

"Every Sunday, we set aside the full day to do a family day activity. We always had our family meeting first to set the tone, and then we paired up to allow a team of two to choose an activity for that day. We committed at least $100 so that the activities would not be restricted by cost. An adventuresome and rewarding activity was to become tourists in our own town. To do so required that we think like a visiting tourist would think and do whatever he or she would do. We went to Waikiki and got those tourist booklets as well as pamphlets from the airport. There were so many things that we had never done even though we had lived here for 15 years. We just took so much for granted, thinking we could always do that later. But later never came. We got entertainment books to get discounts and coupons. This helped. We did the IMAX, Polynesian Cultural Center, Waimea Falls, Paradise Park, hiking trails, and so many beautiful and wonderful experiences that were sitting here right under our noses that we never would have done. It is important to remember that you don't have to spend money to have a great family day. Some of our most memorable times were the stay-at-home days when we played games, like charades, or did skits and recorded ourselves. It is so great to have those videos to reflect on." —Ed

In today's world, everyone lives at such a fast pace. Technology has improved drastically and we can receive information in a matter of seconds. Children do not always have to wait for things. They have the idea that instant gratification is normal. Technology has also made our entire world speed up. It seems like many people are overworked and are constantly running to their next meeting or obligation. We see children participating in numerous activities and becoming booked every night with sports, dance, piano lessons, and then homework. Although it is important to encourage children to be involved, parents do need to consider what kind of effect this has on the child and the family. Is it truly a benefit to them and are they enjoying it? If so, the activities are probably a positive part of their life. Facing this in the real world, can you still make Family Days work? The answer is yes, but it takes tough choices. Adults have to agree that no appointments, social meetings, or work will interfere. Children have to choose activities where no practice, lessons, or games will interfere. If an occasional event falls on Family Day, you can make that the focus and build the day around it. However, many families today are trying to limit activities for their children. Some are allowing them to choose only one or two per semester. These families want to have more family time together. In this family time, they can develop their own play dates, even including sports in the process so that they are all getting exercise. Planning these days can be a lot of fun for everyone. Family play days could be a day of board games, football, baseball, scavenger hunts, skits, hiking, and many more. Children are taught about rules, how to treat and respect siblings, and, most importantly, how to appreciate one another. Younger siblings learn from the older ones and feel important as well.

"Do unto others as you would have them do unto you—the good old Golden Rule. Because everyone was taking turns, each got an opportunity to be the planner. If you wanted your idea to be greeted with great enthusiasm, then you needed to greet everyone else's in the same way. If there was an activity that you really disliked, it was okay to communicate that, but only verbally. You still had to participate exuberantly. If we had let individuals choose whether or not to participate, it would have dissipated and fallen apart. It was one aspect in which nobody had that choice. But the parents did not have to make that requirement. It was how everyone felt when the agreements were set up for how Family Day would work." —Betty

Family togetherness is a way to create unity within the household. When there is unity, there is likely to be more strength. A family represents unity. The members live together, eat together, and grow together. They share the good times and the bad. They always have one another and the home is their refuge and safe haven. It's so powerful when children know that they are loved unconditionally and never put down. They share such an attractive common bond that others want to get in and nobody wants to get out. Effective families will pass this unity on to other parts of the world. It might be in helping others who are in need, or it might be simply by the way they treat others. Our society most definitely needs some of these "family values" spread, as many of us have forgotten the positive aspects of honesty, integrity, forgiveness, generosity, caring, conservation, and respect for life and the earth.

To enhance family unity, we made an agreement that everyone had to at least pretend that they actually wanted to do whatever activity was chosen for the day. I'll never forget when somewhere between two and three years old, it was Molly's turn. She decided that we were going to a park near the ocean to play kickball. Of course, everybody was holding the moan, but had to pretend that they were seriously excited about going to play kickball. Well, we brought the barbeque, we bought steaks, we went down to the park, and we put out bases and started playing kickball as a family. Before you knew it, another family wanted to join us and then another and before it was over, we had attracted a full raging day of kickball with kids of every age from two to probably 14 years old, just having a blast together. We then proceeded to cook our steaks and had a fabulous end to the day. It gave all of us the lesson that it doesn't matter how old you are or what type of game you're playing; if it's really a family activity and you get into it, you will enjoy it. The whole family cannot hold back a smile whenever the thought of that day is brought up." —Ed

What was so great about the good old days? A long time ago (and still today in some cases), the family worked on farms. They were truly unified because they spent all of their time together. They worked for a common goal to produce income and food. Children did not spend hours on television or video games; instead, they had each other. Although some people might argue that these were hard times for our society, the argument might also be made that they were the most stable for our families. People counted on one another and treasured the things they had. It was a time of telling stories about what made each person in the family special, unique, and important. Family interactions required creativity and cooperation. Although everyone worked hard, they loved each other greatly and shared tremendous amounts of quality time. How do we carry the values of those days into the present? Family unity is the secret. It produces children who care about others. It heals pain, suffering, and discomfort. It makes us laugh and enjoy life more. The secret power of unity is strength, which is built up by mutual trust, respect, consideration, caring, faith, and love for one other. It aids in lots of areas, as children know that they always have a safety net that they call home.

Déjà Vu, I'll Never Forget You

Memories, positive and negative, play a huge role in our formation and impact many of the choices that we make in our life. It is important to focus on creating positive memories as building blocks for the future. They might be life changing and serious or very often may be funny things that we look back on and laugh at for years to come. We often learn from these memories as well. Most importantly, they make us appreciate our family even more.

Whether memories come from storytelling, home movies, pictures, or just seeing a familiar place, they engender an emotion that binds us to the other members of our family. They are truly something to cherish and celebrate and can be passed on for generations. Everyone participating in the same event has a different experience, so it's important for the whole family to share memories when creating the family story or history. Sometimes this happens when we're putting pictures into an album or scrapbook. Sometimes it's when we watch old home movies. The key is that memories tell the family's story and talk from the heart.

"It could be just the activity of playing another board game, but what makes it a treasured memory is what happened when we encouraged the older children to lose to younger children. It turned into a great lesson in love on both sides that lasted forever. The older child put aside his or her own pride and unselfishly made the younger child truly believe that he or she had won. It is so rewarding to see the sparkle and twinkle and look of admiration of the younger child looking at the older after a great and hard-fought win. Just recalling the memory of Tony encouraging Molly to make a certain move that gave her the advantage makes my heart burst. These memories also taught all of us that playing the game was way more important than winning." —Betty

No, I Always Sit There

There are many traditions in our world. Religious traditions exist in every religious organization. We also have family traditions that are very important to our lives. As we look back at our own childhoods, we are reminded of traditions in our own past. It might be those special Christmas memories sitting around the piano singing Christmas carols, or it might be the thoughts of cutting down an old-fashioned tree, carrying it home, and stringing popcorn for decoration. The thoughts of going to midnight mass and then returning home to see that Santa had come were truly magical. Simply having a big dinner every Sunday after church might spark some positive memories as well. Holidays often establish traditions over time. However, with so many mixed families today, those traditions might not be as strong. As a result, it is important that we start traditions within our own homes if we have not already done so. If they are already started, think about how you can maintain them. These are precious, wonderful times that cannot be taken away from us. Traditions can be spiritual. We establish them when praying before meals, having special prayer time with our children before bed, and, ultimately, they build important morals and values in our family.

"Why are traditions important for a family, and how do you create them? Traditions are the roots that bind a family. They provide the giant security blanket that says good times will repeat. Kids know that they will have another chance to experience something good, and it is very reassuring. The great thing is that for kids, anything you do twice can become a tradition. Betty and I had very different family, religious, and cultural upbringings. Because of that, we had to create traditions, like the way we would celebrate holidays, or do our famous Waimea Beach breakfast, or just the way we did family days together. I'm so grateful that we learned early the importance of creating traditions rather than thinking that we didn't have any. I love it when our children in their 30's still want to line up and come down the stairs in a special order to start our Christmas day celebration. Also, it is inspiring to see how they have created traditions now for their own families as well."
—Ed

Twenty years from now it might not matter if our house was always clean, the laundry was always caught up, or even if all the yard work was done. It will, however, matter if we spent as much quality time with our children as possible. Further, it will matter if we instilled morals, leadership skills, and respect. It will matter that they look back at their childhood and have positive memories of all the love that surrounded them each day. No, it might not matter what kind of clothes we wore, but it will matter that we made the difference in our children's lives to be sensitive and compassionate citizens on our Earth who can pass that legacy on to their children.

Playing Together and Family Days

Passionate Points

Family days include family meetings, praying and playing together and require a commitment of time and money if they are to be successful. During the specified time, no outside work, no social scheduling conflicts, no boy friends or girl friends, just us.

The topics for family meetings include setting agreements, problem-solving, dreaming or goal setting, menu's for the week and who will cook, ways to support each other, etc. The purpose of meetings is open communication to provide time for each person to be heard, to speak and to be allowed to share in a safe environment without interruption.

Activities on family days need to be packed with play and fun even when you are doing work together. Act like a tourist in your own area, by doing day trips, having picnic's, and hiking. Play outdoor games like kickball, softball, badminton, volleyball, croquet, etc., and indoor games like cards, doing puzzles, board games, charades, skits etc.

Traditions are the glue that bond a family for life. It is easy to create traditions, because anything you do twice can become a tradition as far as kids are concerned.

Dialogue Questions

What am I willing to do to show my commitment to making family days real for us? How does my answer make me feel?

What is one problem that I would like to resolve through a family meeting? How do I feel sharing this with you?

Family Meeting Sharing Questions

(Continue to go around from person to person and make a list for all to see) What are the fun things you would like to do on family days?

What activities have we done as a family that you would like us to keep as a tradition?

Chapter 7

Praise, Thanks, and Forgiveness

If love means never having to say you're sorry, then marriage means always having to say everything twice.

—Estelle Getty

Children are quite funny in that one day they may make you think you're the best parent ever, and the next day they will embarrass you like never before as you carry them kicking and screaming out of a store. Frustration sets in with many parents because they have reached the end of their rope and just don't know what to do. In reality, even if they know how to handle certain situations, they choose differently because of what others may think of them as parents.

Unfortunately, most couples approach parenting as a series of battles to win—the them-against-us war with their children. When highs and lows in our lives are dictated by the behavior of our kids, we have truly missed the joy that parenting is supposed to be. We are allowing our children's behavior to run our lives and ruin our self-image as parents precisely because we focus on and are afraid of what others might be thinking of us. So how do we get off this roller coaster of emotion that we really can't control and give ourselves a chance to feel like successful parents?

Praise and thanks are two of the most powerful fuels to fill the self-image tanks for ourselves as well as for our children. Forgiveness is the quickest way to keep the tanks from draining when we or our kids make mistakes.

Praise and thanks counteract being taken for granted, and forgiveness lets us all be human, have imperfections, and make mistakes. It is unconditional and gives us the chance to start over.

We had been led to believe that too much praise would give our children a big head, but what we discovered is that most people face so much negativity that all the praise and thanks that we could give our children would never make that happen. Those who are boastful are usually the ones who are not hearing it enough from their parents.

It seems that our society encourages success and excellence, but look at what happens to people who attempt to do just that. Take any political candidate, for instance, who sets out to make a difference in the world. Everything is fine until they get under the microscope, and then the criticism and mudslinging begin. Even look at the superstars in sports and see how any little failing is magnified. Even if they choose to avoid media attention, that is criticized. Then bring that down to a classroom with its peer pressure and think about how you are immediately classified as a nerd or a jock if you excel at either academics or sports. The reality is that most people want everyone to be mediocre. For this reason, the home and family need to be the place where praise, thanks, and forgiveness flow generously.

Taking the time to get involved with our kids is also a way to let them know that we care. It may be that kids don't talk to us because they think we're not interested in them or in what they're doing. In truth, they really crave our attention and want us to be an active part of their lives. Now, we know that working full time and maintaining a household can consume every second of the day. When our kids were young, most days we felt like the dots on the *Pac-Man* game. There always seemed to be something chasing after us and gobbling away our time. That is why praise and thanks are so important, because they can be shared on the way to the soccer field or the dance studio or even at the dinner table. As parents, we have the best opportunity to profoundly shape the choices that our children make. An honest praise that demonstrates that we have cared enough to observe something really positive about our child can perk up her ears to hear a message that otherwise might go in one ear and out the other. Believe it or not, you *can* influence your children's decisions, but it takes proactive effort on your part.

Once a child is able to say one word, from that moment on you'll never get to watch another movie, TV show, or do anything else again without a little tot standing over your shoulder asking seven hundred questions a minute. In case you haven't reached that stage yet, here's an example of the time we replaced our fence: "Daddy, why are you digging a hole? How deep does the hole have to be? Mommy, what is Daddy going to do with the dirt when he's done? How come you're putting a steel pole inside? Why are you filling it with that grey stuff? What is concrete? What's a fence? Why do we need fences?" By the end of the day, we wanted to dive in the hole and pour concrete on top of ourselves. Instead of crying uncontrollably and rushing out to the nearest pharmacy to buy earplugs, we strove to use those opportunities for open, honest, one-on-one communication. Before we learned better, we used to say something just to get rid of the child because we were allowing them to be an irritation. What we discovered later is that it was much better to give them a complete answer by pretending that it was an adult neighbor who had asked the question. If the children were not ready for that level, they would grow bored and leave, but if they were getting it, they usually would not ask the same questions over and over, and when they are a little older and you're building something else, you'll have a capable helper.

The example of our little one asking a bazillion questions is pretty benign when compared to some that our teenagers may ask us. If we show them that we're willing to give honest answers at any time—even when the subject makes us uncomfortable—then we'll forge a trusting relationship. Our children will come to us with their concerns because they know we take them seriously. We can't be with our kids 24-7 and protect them from all the peer pressure they face, but we can teach them to deal with it, handle it, and overcome it. Communication gives you insight into your children's world—the sights and sounds that influence them every day. Talking is the primary method that we use to deal with our issues. Our children's peers are their closest and most concrete messengers of society's values. When we get the chance, we need to decide whether we will stand up and live by our own Christian values, which have stood the test of time, or if we will allow ourselves to be swayed by society's standards, which vacillate and change by current whims.

"When I think of helping our kids with peer pressure, several points come to mind. First was sharing our own peer pressure stories. For Betty, it was being coerced into giving an answer on a test and getting caught. For me, one was leaving the school campus in the middle of the school day and having to pay the penalty, and another was speeding in a car with friends, skidding out of control, and seeing my life flash before my eyes. Another step in dealing with peer pressure is talking about the kids' own experiences when they happen and being clear about not only what they were feeling, but also what the others may have been feeling. A last step was setting up protection in advance. We always set and announced a curfew when they were older and could go out on dates. We knew and they knew that they could break the curfew with our permission, but when they called to ask if they could stay out longer or go somewhere else that had not been planned, we simply asked, 'Do you want us to pick you up now?' This gave them the opportunity to say yes or no. I remember times when our children got out of being in cars with drunk drivers or situations in which fights were ready to break out. It is so great and even life-saving to have clear and concise plans set up in advance to give your kids an escape mechanism." —Ed

It is critical to find the right time to talk to teens about peer pressure. You should never have the conversation in front of their friends or yours and should not do it when they are distracted by something that really interests them. When you do detect the right time, encourage them with phrases such as "That's interesting" or "I didn't know that" and by asking follow-up questions like "Is there something else you want to say?" or "Is there anything that you need to tell me?" These questions can be especially powerful if you ever get inside information from a friend or teacher about something that your child has done. Ask the question and see if your child volunteers the topic, then gently lead them to let them know that you know. They will immediately want to know how you found out, and you can just say, "I have my ways." In these conversations you can steer the topic to what types of pressures they may be experiencing. Living and making real your strong Christian values in your own life and asking them to do the same is the most concrete way we know to give your kids a solid foundation. This is the best preventive method to help them know how to act when confronted with a difficult choice. If they can learn to deal positively in this situation when they're young, they are set for life.

Pillow Fight!

Several years ago there was a commercial in which a group of little girls were having a pillow fight. Laughter and feathers were everywhere, and all of a sudden the dad barged through the door and yelled, "Are you guys having a pillow fight?!" Frightened, the little ladies looked at each other and then at their dad. The camera turned to him, and he said, "And you didn't invite me?!" He jumped in the middle and the pillow fight resumed. The intention of this ad was to demonstrate the need for parents to spend more quality time with their kids. Why is it that we as parents are so insistent on catching our kids doing something wrong? Wouldn't it be better to focus our energies on what they are doing right? One of our strongest ideals that we adopted from Spenser Johnson's books *The One Minute Mother* and *The One Minute Father* is to capture kids doing things right instead of always catching them doing things wrong. Once you get in the habit of doing this, you become very conscious of all the good your kids do. For example, your focus shifts to them putting a pair of socks in the hamper rather than their underwear and jeans on the bathroom floor. Through our experience of doing this, we noticed vast improvements in our home.

When you catch your kids doing something right, instead of having the common mind-set of catching them doing something wrong, you imprint or engrain in them the qualities, behaviors, and actions that make them special and unique. Instead of harping on the opposite and getting them focused and dwelling on what they are doing wrong, they spend time in their head developing and dwelling on what else they can do to get more approval. The more they hear what is positive about themselves, the more they live out those qualities, and then their character, values, and self-esteem are enhanced.

What's for Dinner? Chicken Fillets and a Heaping Side of Praise

Our world is so filled with negativity. When kids are playing together at school, they often find ways to cut each other down. They point out the bad, laugh at mistakes, and rarely notice something positive. It is so easy for us to get sucked into gossiping, nagging, and complaining about each other. You always hear comments like "He thinks a lot of himself." But you seldom hear a remark like "He is so much better than he gives himself credit." Even family dynamics can be unintentionally structured to provide a stream of negativity. For instance, there are dominant character traits based on birth order that each child takes on to be special. If the first child takes on good, the second one usually needs to take on bad or vice versa. But the good one is always pointing out the bad one's behaviors. It was so important to understand this when we decided that our home would be a refuge. It kept us and our children focused on avoiding criticism and other negative tendencies inside our family. We all believed that we could not praise each other enough to counter what we might receive in the outside world.

Praise is essential not only to this chapter, but to life. Sometimes we think our society is so much like a bunch of crabs in a bucket, pulling each other back in if one tries to get out. As kids grow, it is important to notice their unique tendencies and character traits and make them aware through praise and recognition. For example honesty, willingness to share or help, compassion, and kindness are such important characteristics to reveal to your children. Remember, it only takes one short acknowledgement at the right moment to get a lifetime of results. We wanted our house to feel safe and secure, a place where the kids didn't have to be on guard all the time. It is absolutely imperative to make the conscious decision to praise your kids consistently and genuinely. This helps to keep the negativity that they receive on the playground or in the classroom out of your home.

It's never too early to start the habit of praise. And you can never give a child too much. One time we were waiting to be seated for dinner and overheard the conversation of the young couple sitting beside us. The little boy must have been around five and was just learning to count to 100. Each time he finished, his mom would tell him how smart he was. Finally, the dad chimed in and said, "Don't keep telling him that; he'll get a big head and won't have any friends at school." We had to bite our lips to keep form saying anything. It's true that people, including children, can get prideful and boastful, but it is better to live with confidence than with insecurity, which could potentially prevent them from living a happy life.

"As young parents we were cautioned into believing that too much praise is bad. But catching kids doing things right can't be beat. I love how Elijah (our grandson) loves how we clap for him when he puts the baby powder back where it belongs or closes a door, and he does it over and over to get that reaction. There is no such thing as enough praise. It shows that you care and pay attention to what they do." —Betty

Praising and rewarding our children's behavior helps them establish strengths and interests that build their self-esteem. A healthy self-esteem leads to generosity, kindness, compassion, and many other virtues. People who fit into the "big head" category actually have poor self-esteem. One important fact is that praise has to be genuine. Empty praise cannot be given to those who are not praiseworthy.

The world is a tough place and kids need all the encouragement and recognition they can get. When we emphasize what our children do right instead of focusing on what's wrong, they learn to feel good about themselves, and they develop self-confidence. Praise can also help to diffuse a tense situation. When you are arguing and having a frustrating time with someone, for example, you can totally change the atmosphere by pointing out to them a praise of appearance, quality, or action. Let's take the example of doing a puzzle with a small child. The variety of shapes and sizes of the pieces can be quite a challenge for the tot, and many times he'll get irritated and start to throw a fit. Praise the fact that he knows which shapes don't fit rather than focusing on how many pieces he's successfully put in the puzzle. Praise changes the mood, and with older kids and adults in particular, it catches them off guard and refocuses the entire situation.

"For me, the prime example for this is driving in the car. Kids are in the back, and Betty and I are in the front, engrossed in our conversation or listening to the radio. At first the kids are fine, then the nudging, slapping, and nagging start. When we were not conscious about this concept, the next thing we would notice was an all-out war going on in the back. This would instantly cause feelings of frustration and anger to well up, and one of us would be yelling for quiet. What a paradox: yelling for quiet. What a relief when we became conscious of the concept, and at the first sign of the initial nudge or nag, we would simply think of something positive and say it. 'Jenny,

you were so good at getting yourself up today all by yourself, and thanks for making sure that Tony was up.' Or, 'Tony, you found your shoes so fast today because you put them on the rack last night.' Or, 'Kelly, thanks for sharing your cupcake with Molly.' All simple, genuine praise for something recent. And it doesn't have to be for something they did, necessarily. 'Chrysy, you must feel so beautiful in your new outfit.' All of these instantly change the mood, and 90 percent of the time, just one gets you an extra ten minutes of peace and quiet. This makes me feel so grateful. Such a small change, such a big result." —Ed

Gratitude, Not Platitude

One of the most annoying things is when you're walking in or out of an establishment and you hold the door for someone and they walk right past you without saying thank you. It's irritating when it's a person that you don't know, but it hurts when it happens with people you know and love. Those two small words take just a moment to say, yet so many of us don't say them. A daily or even hourly dose of thanks is perfect for avoiding one of the greatest relationship sins—taking for granted. It's ironic that most people think the best way to avoid taking the other person for granted is to have a fifty-fifty relationship, but the truth is that it can lead to keeping score and resentment. We know that a fifty-fifty relationship is inadequate. By keeping track, we eventually get to the point where we say, "I do everything for you; you do nothing for me." It has to be each person giving 100% without being concerned about how much the other person gives. Generous portions of thanks and gratitude help us avoid slipping back to the fifty-fifty attitude.

"When we think of all of the things for which we are so grateful—our love for each other, our beautiful children and grandchildren, our friends and our home—passion and excitement overwhelm our hearts." —Ed and Betty

We have gone to many seminars where it has been taught that gratitude needs to start your day. We have found this to be true. Gratitude keeps you on the positive side of life. If you constantly look at what you don't have, you will find it. Keeping at least a mental list of all that God has given you will keep your outlook on life positive. The attitude of gratitude frees you to be other-centered so that you are able to praise, thank, and forgive. Aren't the things that you crave basic needs? If thankfulness is not a basic need (psychologically speaking), it should be. Because we are human we all need to know that what we have done is appreciated, or we might lose heart. It is important to have self-gratitude, but for most of us, that's not enough. We like to hear it concretely from others, especially our spouses. Marriage is the training or proving ground of giving. But there just comes a moment when you give, give, give, and realize that no one has said, "Thank you so much." You get hurt, and that feeling triggers a glitch in the unconditional love and unconditional giving mode. You judge that you have been taken for granted and it hurts.

Each of us gets so caught up in everyday life and usually just slip into our roles. We get barraged from outside by requests from kids and calls from friends, and we can't just ignore them, so we handle them in addition to our normal activities. If you and your spouse are like us, one of us asks the other, "Did you remember to do [whatever]?" And then the accusations start to fly: "Why didn't you do that?" or "I only have two hands; I'm not a superhero!" But when we make a conscious effort to be aware of what each other is doing and remember to say thank you, it helps us to realize and understand the sacrifices that we make for each other. This way there is no score keeping, and that little "thanks" totally dissipates any mounting frustration.

Our family motto is "We are so blessed and fortunate." We've said it so often that it became a family joke, and we can already see the smirk on our kids' faces as they read this. But if you were to ask any one of them about their childhood, each one of them would tell you that they never in a million years would trade the tough times that we got through together; in fact, they cherish them. Now remember, all eight of us lived in a 900-square-foot, three-bedroom, one-bath house! Believe us when we say that eight is truly enough! During that time, they were young enough that none of them ever wished for a separate room, even when they all slept side-by-side like sardines on the floor in the same room.

As a matter of fact, when we previously had a bigger house with beds for all of them, they slept side-by-side on the landing between the bedrooms instead of in their own beds. Having the attitude of gratitude that "we are so blessed and fortunate" allowed us to use the tough times to bond. Just think of how much forced communication went on when everyone was in the same room sleeping on futons, picking them up every morning in order to get dressed for school, versus sleeping in separate bedrooms. Gratitude allowed us to see the good and make the best of it. It could have been so easy to compare ourselves to others who had their own bedrooms and we could have been very miserable about our condition.

When you and your family carry an attitude of gratitude, the attitude becomes infectious and everyone wants to be a part of it. The kids' friends always wanted to come over to our house. Showing and sharing gratitude is the cornerstone for a positive attitude. It starts with being thankful for ordinary things, like sunrises and sunsets; the fresh, clean smell after a rain; or the feeling of raindrops on your face. Even thanks for just being able to get out of bed and get to the bathroom by yourself. Thanks for the parking place. Thanks for a kid scoring a goal. Everything good or bad happens for a reason, so learn to say thank you for anything and everything in your life.

True Forgiveness

Whenever we step on each other's toes, either by word or deed, we need to seek forgiveness so that we don't destroy the close relationships in our family. Often we tell our children, "Say you're sorry!" And then we notice that those words can morph into a sarcastic "Sor-ry" with no heartfelt meaning behind it. What is the difference between "I'm sorry" and "Please forgive me"? The bottom line is that "Please forgive me" needs two people, and "I'm sorry" only needs one. It is really critical in a relationship to realize that anything you do that does not involve the other still involves the other. Saying "I'm sorry" can make you feel good, but it is really selfish. "Please forgive me" is other-centered because it gives the injured person the opportunity to give you the gift of forgiveness when they are ready to do so, which could be immediate or delayed. Asking for forgiveness is even more powerful when it is specific. For instance, "Will you please forgive me for agreeing with all of the kids and abandoning or betraying you in front of them? You must have felt hurt, alone, like being stabbed in the back." This way, the injured person knows what the hurt was all about and that you knew what it was also. It makes them feel like you really know what was going on and that you cared enough to compassionately ask for forgiveness.

Hurt and pain in a relationship are so difficult because they can be inflicted without our knowledge. Although there are times during a heated argument when we can attempt to hurt each other, the unintentional hurts usually happen because of breakdowns in the relationship over long periods of time. These types of hurt are subtle and are usually caused when we feel taken for granted or used. The intentional hurts in an argument are usually instantaneous and razor sharp and based on anger and resentment. Regardless of how they occur, hurts are determined by the perception of the injured person. There are many times when we are clueless about the fact that our spouse or children have gotten their feelings hurt. There is a great temptation at these times to become self-righteous and let pride prevent you from even seeking forgiveness.

"I remember the time I told Betty how beautiful her hair looked and witnessed the smile fade from her face as she became quiet and distant. I asked her what was wrong, and she simply said that she heard me say that her hair usually looks bad and that she was feeling hurt. At first I could not believe my ears and buried myself in my work stewing over the whole situation. Finally I realized that I had been working long hours and spending little time paying attention to her. I realized that my compliment surfaced her feelings of being taken for granted. I had barely noticed her, so my compliment stood out like a sore thumb. I asked Betty to forgive me for not paying attention and complimenting her regularly. I watched that beautiful smile return to her face as she reached out to hug me. Later she shared that she was even feeling guilty and confused for reacting the way she did. My being able to ask for forgiveness opened the door for both of us to grow to a new level in our relationship." —Ed

Granting forgiveness can often be even more difficult than asking for it. How can we practice granting forgiveness to keep our relationships firm? Forgiving is in the heart of the offended. We often think of forgiveness as something that someone who has done us wrong must ask of us. Refusing to forgive by holding on to the anger, resentment, and a sense of betrayal can be selfish and make your own life miserable. It's much easier to grant forgiveness when you think that you have been listened to, but at times it just takes a decision to love and trust again. This simply means listening beyond the words. How often is it that words cannot express our experience? Just think about trying to describe a special sunset. Usually that cannot be done. This is true also when trying to share hurt or problems in the relationship. Unless you listen with the heart and go beyond the words and really tune in to the person, you wouldn't know what that hurt must have felt like to him or her. With children it is especially important to listen beyond the words because they often don't connect feelings with what they are saying.

Healing is the only way to prevent past injuries and hurts from recurring. Healing has to be conscious, and it doesn't just happen unless true forgiveness is involved. When you have a cut, you can stop the bleeding and put on a Band-Aid, but it can take weeks for the scar to heal; additionally, if it is not cared for with antibiotics and cleaned and maintained, it can even become infected and flare up again. The same is true with hurt in a relationship. Lavishing love and actually making a change for the other person can sometimes be the lotion that totally heals the wound and settles the heart.

"Why do we practice praise, thanks, and forgiveness? They color the way we are in our daily life and affect the way we approach all of the other parenting techniques. Unless we are conscientious, we can so easily go through life being in our own selfish little world. We have to really think about what is going on with each member of our family. How am I affecting her? What are his needs? How can I contribute to making others feel better about themselves, etc.? We can sit and just stare at the TV and not pay attention to what's going on around us at all. Or we can focus on praising, thanking, and asking forgiveness so that we stay aware, alive, and other-centered, which brings true joy into parenting." —Ed and Betty

Chapter 7
Praise, Thanks and Forgiveness

Passionate Points

Sincere praise confirms and empowers others to believe in their own unique abilities, character traits and value. There is no such thing as too much praise. Learning how to accept praise is just as important as giving it.

Thanks is the antidote for the greatest relationship sin which is taking for granted.

Kids feel fearful and anxious when they see you fight, but they feel safe and secure when they see the whole process of fighting, healthy discussion, forgiveness and healing.

Dialogue Questions

What is my favorite thing about us as a couple? How does my answer make me feel?

Describe a hurt or situation where I said I'm sorry, but know I need to ask your forgiveness? How do I feel sharing this with you?

Family Meeting Sharing Questions

(Put one member of the family in a seat in the middle of the sharing circle), everyone else share what you like best about that person.

What are you most grateful for in your life right now?

Chapter 8

Kids Are a Resource, Not a Burden

Always be nice to your children because they are the ones who will choose your rest home.

—Phyllis Diller

Any new mother who remembers that overwhelming feeling of love after looking at that precious miracle from God knows the impact that a child has on a family. Children are truly sent to us to make a difference in the world. Not only will they someday be an active part of society, but they are a true blessing sent straight from Heaven. Only time will let us know if the child will be a teacher, a plumber, a doctor, or a banker. The possibilities are endless for our children of today. Of course, there are many years from that precious moment of birth until they are out on their own. These years in between are another gift from God that parents are given. God allows *us* to care for them, inspire them, and mold them into fine humans for our future generations. What an honor!

Although most parents know that they are so fortunate to have children, they, themselves, are only human. The trials and tribulations of raising a child sometimes get the best of all of us. Parents worry about financial issues, careers, and common everyday life situations. They help children get to various activities, counsel them when they are sad or angry, play nurse when they are sick, and play teacher when they need guidance with homework. With all of these pressures, it is no surprise that parents sometimes get tired and frustrated. Some may even think of their children as a constant responsibility, which leads to seeing them as a burden. It is during these times that we need to take a step back and think about children being a resource instead. Kids can be a resource emotionally by giving us love and affirmation, and physically by helping with goals, projects, and activities both in and out of the house.

"If you are looking for problems you will find them. If you're looking for solutions, you will find them, too. It is so hard in our society because of our birth-control mentality. We see fertility as a problem, and therefore conception is a problem, and kids get a bad rap before they are even conceived. After birth, it's quite frequent that we hear 'Take your crying baby out of here. What kind of responsible parent are you?' Everyone makes sure that you know it is your responsibility. That's why it is so easy to forget that children are also a joy and a resource. It is so exciting that it still works with grandchildren. You should have seen me with them yesterday. You wouldn't believe how fast we moved all the groceries out of the car. One at a time, they came to me and asked for stuff. I just handed it to them. The next thing I knew, it was all piled up in front of the door to the house. Of course, that was not ideal, but how much easier is it to put everything away from there instead of making five trips to the car. I wish I could grab and shake every parent to help them see this now. It really isn't quicker to do it yourself, thinking that they are not capable, because allowing kids to be a resource is part of your one-on-one quality time with them. It is never a waste. It is a way to kill two birds with one stone. You're teaching the kids something valuable. As time goes on, this will actually help you save time, but you're also taking advantage of that special moment when you're showing them how important they are to you one-on-one. It's just fabulous." —Ed

Children can help in the family in so many ways. Not only are they a resource, but they can make simple chores seem like so much fun. Parents can find joy in watching kids make a normal boring thing like sweeping the porch or folding laundry turn into a game. Children will feel important if they get to help, and parents will see them as a true benefit instead of a burden. Families can use this time to talk and open up the lines of communication. It is also just good quality time together without the television, video games, or other distractions. Parents find it amazing that even a two-year-old can help with putting laundry in the correct drawers, wiping down a counter, or carrying in an item from the grocery store.

Wouldn't our world be so much better if everyone focused on finding good qualities in children? What if we see a young parent struggling in the store with three screaming children? We should not judge or criticize. If we point the finger and make comments about how the mother should be more responsible for the actions of the kids, we are only causing more negativity toward children. Any parent who has been in this situation knows how embarrassing it can be. On the other hand, if we can empathize with her and show care and patience toward young children, maybe other people will notice and do the same in a similar situation. We could even offer to help by pushing a basket, grabbing some groceries off the shelf for her, or conversing with the kids to entertain them briefly. A kind word and gesture from a stranger showing support to our young generation can work miracles.

The same is true with our teenagers. Too often, people focus on the clothes they wear, the words they speak, and the music they listen to. We forget that teenagers are trying to find their place in the world. They are seeking to find that identity through various ways. Although it might look strange to all of us, it is their entire world. Teenagers often get a bad rap from our society. There are many young adults who do show respect toward others. They show that they can be a resource to our society by volunteering time to charities, helping their peers who are struggling, and even helping care for their younger siblings in single-family homes. Most of us do not focus on these positive factors enough; we find it easier to judge and criticize.

"The couple is the heart of the family. We learned this concept at a convention we went to when the children were quite young, and it set the tone for our attitude from then on regarding how Ed and I were the core of our family. We also discovered at this convention that if we think of our kids as a responsibility, it can turn them into a burden. Instead, we focused on them being a resource, and it exploded the possibilities for making everyday life more adventuresome. We asked them for advice and even asked for their input about spending money and about finances in general. We worked together to come up with their consequences. We asked them to do their own laundry and take care of more chores. Once we were on a camping vacation, and when we pulled up to a site, Ed and I sent the kids off to play while we prepared dinner and got settled for the night. We ended up eating way too late with lots of grouchiness flying around. What a shift when we all stood

in a line and passed the supplies from one person to the next. That helped us move the stuff in the camper from the front to the back in record time, and the brigade was born in our life. Now the brigade is used to bring groceries in from the car and even for huge chores like carrying household goods to the moving van. Using this concept makes everyone a resource, the jobs get done more quickly, and the whole family benefits and even has fun!" —Betty

Kids are going to make mistakes. They are kids! They are learning each and every day. Their brains are still developing, and they don't always make smart, rational decisions. This is part of the growing process. It is trial and error. We learn best when we try something many times. Sometimes the hardest and best achievements are the ones that took years of practice. What gets in the way of letting our kids experience this learning process is that parents often believe that they are judged by how their kids behave. Although we are here to guide our children in making good choices, we cannot be with them 24 hours a day and make every decision for them. We can model and try to instill morals, values, and love in them with the hope they will choose the right path. However, we have to be there for them on the other side with support and reassurance if the choice they made is poor. The reality is that we as parents are not perfect and neither is any child. Parents do want their children to be successful no matter what the circumstance, but we have to be understanding and patient as well.

"I think the bottom line for seeing kids as a resource is expectation, which ties into attitudes. If you have the expectation of burden, then it is so overwhelming a burden that it is crushing and no fun at all. It's just a job and work. Expecting a responsibility? Then it goes back to the attitude of your kids being a reflection on you, and if they are not perfect, then you are a terrible parent. But, when they are a resource, the attitude of the parent is that they are a necessary contributing component of the community of the family. This unique individual impacts the family in ways that no one else can. The parent gets to think up ways to utilize the talents, capabilities, and genius of this great being. We loved designing fun ways to keep our home organized with chore charts and yard projects and lots of rewards and positive affirmations. I feel so charged up about this. It's just a creative and fun way to parent." —Betty

Even Young Children Can Have Responsibility

"It is important to realize that young children are much more capable of being responsible than we give them credit." —Betty

Young children want to be a part of the family by helping out around the house. They are capable of doing many things that we do not even realize. If we allow them to participate, they feel successful and wanted. They learn so much from watching older brothers and sisters. Children as young as two years old can sit in the laundry room (with the help from siblings or parents) and pour a scoop of detergent into the washer, get clothes out of the dryer, and even fold items such as washcloths. Often, parents are so overwhelmed with everything they have to accomplish each day that they cannot see the big picture. Many of those accomplishments can be taken care of with the help of the children. It might not be the most efficient use of time but the special one-on-one opportunity makes up for what some might think a waste. Establishing routine and clear expectations for each family member will ease the load for parents while teaching the children vital life skills by setting up chores that the kids are responsible for each day or week.

"It is obvious that if you are looking for burdens and responsibility, you will find burden and responsibility. But when you are looking for resource, you will find that, too. I had a great experience of our 15-month-old grandson as a resource. In the morning when I fixed our fruit smoothie, he was always there to assist me in turning on the blender. I was in a hurry and was a little relieved to see that he was not around when I started putting ingredients into the pitcher, but as I was just about to finish, I felt that little hand on my leg and quickly picked up Elijah and put him on the counter next to the blender to turn it on. Instead of flipping the switch, he pointed past the blender. I said, 'Elijah, I don't have time to play today; just turn it on,' but he defiantly sat there pointing past the blender to the stove. Finally, I looked where he was pointing and saw the top to the pitcher, which I had forgotten. I screamed with such thankfulness that I probably frightened poor Elijah to death, but as soon as I put the top on the blender, he flipped the switch. What a fabulous resource that child was in saving me unbelievable amounts of clean-up time, not to mention probably a new outfit for the day." —Ed

There is also a fine line between seeing children as a resource and making them feel used or taken for granted. It is important to make sure that the kids have a voice and that they are taken seriously. But every once in a while, it is good for us parents to get away with pulling a fast one!

"We had been very, very busy doing a lot of charity work, and a lot of the work did require that we leave kids at home in the evening. Jenny and Tony were old enough to babysit, so we just took advantage of that fact and frequently left the kids when we had to go to a meeting. At one of our family meetings, the kids announced that they resented being taken for granted; they thought that we should at least ask and give them the option instead of assuming that they wanted to babysit. So, we made the agreement, and for several weeks, everything worked out fine, until we got a last-minute call late in the afternoon and needed to leave to go out to an emergency meeting. Well, we asked the kids if they would be willing to babysit, and Jenny announced that she was not, so we asked Tony and he said no, too. We then went right down the line: Kelly, no; Danny, no; Chrysy, no; and finally Molly, the youngest at three years old, said, 'Yes, I will.' So we handed her the $11, and Betty and I said, 'Thank you, sweetheart. Love all you guys, have a good time,' and we walked out the door and went to our meeting. All the way to the meeting, we just laughed out loud when we thought about the looks on their faces leaving the littlest in charge of all of them. Of course, we knew they would take care of each other, but it was one of our real triumphs as parents in which we didn't live up to our promise and yet got away with one." —Ed

Attitude is one of our greatest inner strengths. We can start each morning with the choice of our attitude. We can think positively and think things will be all right no matter what comes our way, or we can think negatively and start out with a chip on our shoulder. Only we have control over how we look at life. We also choose our attitude toward our children. If we expect them to make messes all day, talk back to us, and be disrespectful, that is likely what we will get from them. On the other hand, if we let them know their own possibilities, they can shine. Children are capable of so many wonderful ideas, thoughts, and dreams. It is up to us to give them the space to let their positive creativity come through.

"One of the most important guidelines for Ed and me was to be fair with each child and keep things equal or proportionate between them. We wanted to be fair about what we expected of them and fair with their privileges. Our expectations were based on what we thought they were capable of, and usually they exceeded our expectations because they loved to be needed and surprise us with their abilities. If chores or privileges were based on age, then we really had to be consistent with the younger children so that the older ones did not feel cheated. If older children were tall enough to go on a ride at the amusement park, we didn't hold them back just because the younger ones might feel left out. But we always included the younger ones and let them participate as much as they could. This let them know what they had to look forward to. Because younger children had the modeling of the older ones, we saw them become capable at an earlier age than did their older siblings. Our experience taught us many things. The support in a family allows children to flourish at any age. The guidelines published about what children are supposed to be able to do at different stages sometimes boxes them in. Even a two-year-old wants to be independent by nature, so we learned to capitalize on that and always gave them something to do." —Betty

Label Their Lunch Boxes, Not Them

For children to be true resources, they need to be allowed to flourish as individuals, experiment with various personality traits, and not be boxed in by birth order or labels that parents might assign them. There is a difference between pointing out that Jenny loves to read and Chrysy loves to play soccer, versus labeling Jenny as a reader and Chrysy as an athlete. Labels pigeonhole a child and make it difficult to change. When Chrysy really wanted to excel in academics instead of sports, she was able to make that shift. Parents need to be very sensitive in how we treat our children. Although the oldest is often a leader, we cannot put more responsibilities on that person. They will begin to resent this and feel like they are being taken advantage of in the family. The same is true with the youngest. If we baby him all of the time, it will be much more difficult for him to gain knowledge and become independent.

In a family each child craves attention from Mom and Dad. To get that attention, their behaviors can be positive or negative, because the means justifies the end when it comes to feeling a sense of belonging for a child. It does not matter to children what they have to do to be seen as special and noticed apart from other siblings. They will do whatever it takes. Children at various stages of their development assume a group of character traits that make them unique and special. If they display these traits long enough, they will be labeled as having that personality.

"The bottom line is that 90 percent of the time, the first child takes the trait of good and will make sure that you know the second is bad—but how do the next children in larger families find uniqueness? They adopt other predominant character traits like charming, stupid, cute, and scholar. It does not mean that this is what the child is. For instance, in our family, Dan, the fourth, probably had one of the highest IQs, but if you asked him to take out the garbage, he would say, 'What garbage? I don't know how.' I wanted to strangle him. I'd hear the words in my head getting ready to say, 'Over there, stupid!' But I bit my tongue to not say it, because words like that are exactly how permanent labels are formed." —Ed

We, as parents, need to recognize that there might be tendencies for the "good" child to keep the "bad" child "bad." He or she might point out that the other one did not do well on his report card and spilled his milk at the dinner table. This child might point the finger, find fault, and place blame whenever possible. That is the operating procedure of the good child. Parents must override it whenever possible. "I know that Tony spilled his milk, but look at how well he ate his vegetables so he can grow up big and strong." We want to make sure that this dynamic is broken and splintered and not allowed to really become a label; it should not be anything more than just the characteristic for uniqueness.

"The good child keeps the bad child bad. Why? Each child, not just the good child, wants to keep his or her uniqueness alive and well. They don't want to lose their identity in the shuffle of daily life. Good and bad are the first two and most pronounced. Also, this is most relatable to a society in which having two children is the norm. Good is on the path to please the parents. He or she follows directions, does his or her best at everything like school and sports, and helps around the house. Bad has his or her own agenda with

tuning out directions (didn't hear you), has problems at school, and can't stand to do chores. Good helps bad be bad by

(1) withholding information or directions given by the parents, or

(2) being certain to inform the parents when bad hasn't done what he or she is supposed to do or has acted in an inappropriate way." —Betty

Although the characteristics that go along with birth order are necessary for each child to gain uniqueness in the family, we still have to be cautious to keep it from becoming a permanent label. If we expect our oldest to always act as the smartest, be a leader, and be outgoing, we might pigeonhole them into living those characteristics even if that is not who they really are. Then if she acts shy or does poorly at something, our expectations as parents are not met, and we get frustrated or disappointed when she is just really being her true self. It is important to let children develop their own personality.

"Each child wants to be unique and special in the family. Probably the worst thing for a kid to hear is, 'You're just like your brother,'—just like it would be hard to swallow for a second wife or husband to hear, 'You're just like my first wife (or husband).' We all have ingrained in our being, planted by God, that we are not like anyone else in the world. Amazing! And lovely! We like to belong to our family unit and be a unique family, but each individual wants to have special capabilities and gifts and talents within that unit." —Betty

What Do You Think?

Children love to make decisions at home, at school, or with their friends. They make many of the same decisions that we as adults make: what to eat and wear, and whether or not to follow someone's advice. But unfortunately, some parents don't allow their children to make their own decisions. This may be out of fear. Many parents may make decisions because they think they know what's best for the kids or because they aren't sure that their kids will make good decisions. There are great benefits in training kids to become good decision makers by allowing them to do so whenever possible. They learn to think for themselves, find out what works best for them, begin to trust themselves, become responsible for their lives, and gain confidence in their ability to make wise decisions.

One of the best ways to do this is to incorporate children as a resource in making family decisions. If the children are included in this process, they will be more likely to participate, understand things at a deeper level, and learn give and take. Negotiation skills will be learned and applied in other areas of their lives. The prime place to bring up family decisions is at family meetings. Should we sell this house and move closer to town? What high school do you want to attend? Should we buy a new car? Where should we go for vacation, and should it be at Christmas time or summer? What color should we paint the house? What consequence should we have for breaking a family rule? What should we set as a family rule? Which activity should we attend on a day when there is a conflict of activities? What is bedtime for children at what age? What is curfew for dates? When kids have a stake in these decisions and others, there is so much more cooperation and they rarely spend time figuring out how to break rules. There is little, if any, argument, and it really works until it doesn't, and then you decide as a family to redo it and the cycle continues.

Remember that all decisions have consequences both positive and negative. We parents have in most cases learned to connect the dots. For instance, we know that excessive drinking of alcohol can leave us miserable the next day. We also know that we will do better in anything that we attempt after a good night's sleep. Kids in many cases still need to learn how to connect consequences to their decisions. The ultimate goal is for them to be able to think through the consequence before following through on a decision. In order for our children to learn this, we need to point out the consequence for the decisions that our children make whenever possible. For instance, "Aren't you proud of the terrific score you made on that exam? I'm so proud of your decision to go to bed early to get a good night's rest so you could be alert and at your best to take the exam."

When children are involved in making decisions, there is much more support, participation, and even action on their part in carrying out the decision. When we talk through and model our decisions or guide them with their decisions, we provide the learning situation that is vital in order for them to know how decisions are made.

Here's a Cookie; Now Give It Back

Rewards are a big part of life. Adults get rewarded with a paycheck if they go to their jobs, do well, and show up on time. Students in school get rewarded with a good grade for doing their work, studying for tests, and participating in class. Athletes get rewarded by winning if they practice hard, listen to the coach, and follow the game plays. Children in families love to be rewarded as well. Instead of punishing kids for doing a poor job at something, we can focus on the good things and give praise and rewards. This is a family process that includes everyone from young to old.

The difference between rewards and punishments as an incentive is night and day. There are two types of rewards: parent-imposed and child-earned. Parent-imposed means that the child does something like put rubbish in a garbage can, and you notice and praise. Child-earned means that you set up a chore chart and the children gets a sticker every time she puts something in the garbage. It is much more fun to think up a reward for getting a project or chore accomplished than to think of a punishment if it doesn't get done. For example, as a reward we can say, "When we finish these chores, we will go to the ice cream shop for a shake or sundae." On the other hand, as a punishment, we can say, "If you don't finish these chores, no TV tonight." Which one is more motivational?

Then, there are unplanned, spontaneous rewards like, "Wow, you did all that homework without being told! Do you want to go to a movie?" If homework is a constant problem, think about what would be best: "If you don't do your homework again, no TV tonight," or if you said, "I see you're still having trouble doing your homework. What special treat would you like to have on the weekend if I set up a chart and give you a star for getting your homework done every day next week?" Let them be involved with thinking of the reward and make it fun and positive instead of a negative punishment.

Rewards are so effective for getting a desired behavior. Some people object to the possibility that the kid is acting better only for the reward and not for the intrinsic value of the changed behavior. Another objection is that the word "reward" is a nice word for "bribe," which has lots of nasty connotations. We override those objections with a peaceful, positive, joyful experience that leads to changed behavior. Punishment is a word we never liked. We preferred consequences, logical and natural, which are a much more positive way to correct unwanted behaviors. To motivate kids is a forward-going, positive experience. You don't want punishment, which is a killing, demeaning and stifling experience. After all, parents are in charge of guiding their children to make honest and positive decisions in life. If they learn that it is better to make good choices when they are young, they are more likely to choose good paths for years to come.

Chapter 8
Kids are a Resource, Not a Burden

Passionate Points

Our attitude about our children controls our parenting experience. If we see them as a joy and a resource we will be astounded, and if we see them as a burden and responsibility we will be stressed out.

When we encourage our children to help us make family decisions they feel listened to, capable and needed. They are much more likely to participate and cooperate when they have a stake.

Each child acquires traits to be unique in the family. The traits can be influenced by birth order or any labeling by others including teachers, parents and siblings. If repeated constantly labels will box children in and take away their ability to truly be themselves.

Dialogue Questions

In what ways do I see our children as a joy and a resource? How does my answer make me feel?

In what ways do I see our children as a burden and a responsibility? How does my answer make me feel?

Family Meeting Sharing Questions

Share what specific things need to be done to keep our home clean, uncluttered and a nice place to live. (Use this as the foundation for a chore chart)

Where should we go on our next vacation and what time of year can it be?

At what age should each child start to do his or her own laundry?

Chapter 9

The Importance of Belonging

There is no such thing as fun for the whole family.

—Jerry Seinfeld

"You don't know how I feel, and you don't care," "Leave me alone," "Get out of my space," "I don't need you." If you have ever heard these kinds of comments from your children, then perhaps it's time to stand back and look at what is happening in your family. Ask yourself who or what comes first: your career, family, spouse, God, or yourself? If you don't put God first and at the head of your family, a sense of belonging is impossible because everyone is working toward their own needs instead of the common goal of serving Him. Ultimately, the only one who can meet our need to belong is God. He planted that need in us as a driving force to get us to heaven where we will feel the ultimate belonging!

When husbands and wives experience times of emptiness and aloneness, they often put undue stress on their relationship by thinking it is the other's fault that they feel this lack of belonging. We adults must realize that we cannot expect anyone else, including our spouse, to meet most of our needs. I can choose to love by communicating regardless of how I am feeling. Kids, on the other hand, just react to their feelings, and when they feel insecure, alone, empty, or somehow unattached, they are compelled to act out in ways that will get attention to make sure the parent still cares! The problem for us as parents is that the children get their need to belong met whenever we react to them, and they will use either positive or negative behavior to get that reaction.

The sense that "I belong in this family" is not something children automatically feel. Rather, it is something we orchestrate for them in many ways through the family structure, including one-on-one time, family meetings, playing games, and even tucking them into bed at night. The issue of belonging to the family is really one of building positive bonds of attachment to each other—a healthy aspect of family life. Belonging is a basic, healthy human need. Saying that we belong or appearing to belong are poor substitutes for actually feeling a sense of belonging. The goal of every child, whether he is willing to admit it or not, is to feel that sense of belonging to the parent and the family; otherwise they act out (either positively or negatively) to gain attention. This goes along with the need seeds planted in us at birth, the struggles for survival and for food, clothing, and shelter. God planted these seeds to ensure growth and fuller expression. One of those seeds is the need to belong. As a form of punishment, ancient civilizations would admonish those who broke the law by pretending that the person did not exist. Most would go off and actually die after being ostracized from the group. When children feel separated, they believe that they have to vie for their parents' attention and the results are often disastrous. The undivided attention of a parent means everything to a child, but to a busy parent this need and resulting behavior can be seen as a nuisance and an irritation instead of a top priority.

The need to feel that we belong is compelling. To feel loved, safe, important and secure is fundamental to everyone, regardless of age. It is good to look at that need like a gas tank in a car. As you drive through life, that gas tank gets lower, and we fill it up over and over again. We never want it to get to zero because we would be sitting on the side of the road waiting for help. If a child's "gas tank" of belonging ever gets to zero, you might be in need of professional help. The more that we as parents take opportunities to positively fill our kid's gas tank with praise, undivided instant attention, taking them seriously, and catching them doing something right, the less need they will have to act negatively to get our attention.

*"Why is it that when a sense of belonging is low, kids will do something positive **or** negative to be next to you? The irony of belonging is that children only have to know that you are there for them and that they are important to you. The bad news is that they are getting your undivided attention*

even when you reprimand, spank, yell, or do any other negative reaction to correct the situation. If you react to sassy or disrespectful language, sooner or later you will get it. If you react to rudeness in front of your friends, you will get it. If you react to soiling underwear, to markers on the wall, or to yelling and fighting with other siblings—just wait, you will get it. To a child, your negative reaction is a clear demonstration that you care, and it actually fills their belonging tank! If you can't proactively keep each child's belonging tank full with positive reinforcement like date nights, reading books, playing games, etc., then they will do whatever works to get it full. Better to notice and acknowledge and praise the heck out of the positive than to deal with the negative behavior." —Ed

The need for belonging is a powerful driving force in all of us, but especially in kids, because their primary source for getting that need and all of their needs met is first from the parent and then from the entire family. When the need is met, the child exhibits harmony and cooperation. When the need is absolutely lacking, the child exhibits helplessness and loss of spirit. Anywhere in between, the child is craving attention, and that is why we must ensure that we make time in our busy days to provide special moments for each child.

The Belonging Chart

So then how do we address everyone's needs, including our own? How do we deal with the specific needs of our children without sacrificing our own sanity? It wasn't until we learned the Belonging Chart as taught at the Ho'ala Parenting Classes that we were able to answer these questions. We called the Belonging Chart the game board of life, and it is a great way to approach parenting. For us, this gave us the freedom to enjoy parenting. Before we knew about this, we rated our parenting in a purely self-centered manner. If the kids were good, we were great parents. And if the kids screwed up, which seemed overwhelmingly the case most of the time, we were bad parents. We inaccurately assumed that everyone was judging us based on how our kids behaved. This chart gave us separation and freedom to realize why and when kids cooperated or why and when they didn't. Through our experience, we offer you the Belonging Chart below to help you and your family better understand each other's feelings, what they mean, and what to do about them.

Child's Behaviors	Child's Stream of Consciousness	Adult's Feeling Based on Child's Behavior	Child's Sense of Belonging to Parent
I Cooperate	I'm confident in myself and my abilities. How can I help everyone else?	Pleased	100 percent
I Seek Attention	They're ignoring me, so I have to get their attention to feel accepted.	Annoyed or Irritated	75 percent
I Search for Power	If I don't win or have control, they will think less of me.	Irate or Fuming	50 percent
I Have to Get Even	If I don't get revenge, then I'm a failure.	Hurt	25 percent
I Can't and Won't	I can't do anything right, so that means I'm helpless and worthless.	Hopelessness	0 percent

It's very difficult to know what's going on inside of other people, especially your children, but what makes the chart so attractive is that it starts by just knowing what's going on inside yourself (see third column). If you look at the Belonging Chart as a game board, it provides a graphic way to see that the feeling of belonging is like a gas tank that can be anywhere between 100 percent full and empty. At different levels, the child has a different stream of consciousness. For instance, at 100 percent, a child is saying,

"I'm okay; how can I help others and serve?" At 50 percent, he is saying, "I'm okay if I do something drastic to win their attention." The feeling for the parent when the child feels 100 percent belonging is pleased, peaceful, and harmonious. When the child is reacting at the 50 percent level of belonging, the feeling for the parent is irate, fuming, and angry. When you as a parent notice that you are feeling peaceful, you will see that the behavior of the child who is feeling 100 percent belonging is cooperation and being of service. When you are feeling angry, you will notice a power struggle and confrontation from the child, and you can immediately know that the belonging tank is at 50 percent. By tuning in to how we are feeling as parents, we can instantly determine where the gauge is on our child's belonging tank. It gives us the power to choose what we need to do to remedy the situation.

"The Belonging Chart helped me to see the day-to-day interactions with our children more as a game than a chore. Instead of constantly seeing problems that I had to fix, I started to get in touch with the way I was feeling. In the beginning, I noticed that my parenting style was filled with a lot of anger. But by looking at the chart, I was able to see that my anger was inspired by the bickering and fighting going on among the children. Gradually, instead of yelling, demanding, and becoming a drill sergeant to gain order, I was able to step back and observe to see where the kids were playing on the chart. I could see that they were at the searching-for-power stage, and I knew that their belonging tanks were only half full. When I was really upset, I would just physically remove myself from the situation without saying a word, and half of the time I would notice that the whole situation just evaporated by itself. I was able to notice my own hot buttons, and at times I was astonished at how cleaver kids were to have learned exactly how to push them. After gaining my composure, I could come back in and change the whole mood by just offering to do something like go for a ride or play a game. This was a big key for me to be able to start listening to feelings instead of getting embroiled in the words. It was also reassuring to realize that the lowest on the chart that any of our kids had gone was revenge. Instead of feeling like a failure as a parent, I saw this as a huge success. At least my child was still in the game! When a child reaches assumed helplessness, it usually takes professional guidance to get him or her back on the game board. It was truly amazing to see how quickly my anger was being replaced by more and more peace and harmony." —Ed

"There is just so much to say about the influence of this chart on my decision making. I learned specific steps to move my relationship with each child up the chart. At every level, the key ingredient is to schedule a special time with each child on a regular basis. This continues to nip in the bud any loss in the feelings of closeness. When I realized that a child was anywhere on the chart besides cooperation, I had to control myself and not react to my own feelings. I would then calmly remove myself from the negative situation for a 'me time-out' and then come back to interact with the child in a caring, kind, but firm way." —Betty

Once we understood the power of the Belonging Chart we were better able to address the priorties. The house is a mess. Laundry is scattered everywhere. Does that matter more than whether you have taken time to have a hug? Taken time to check whether or not homework is being done? Taken time to find out if there is a special event coming up that you should attend? It's all about priorities. You don't necessarily have to put them in a definitive order. All can be balanced if you have the right attitude. Have you ever asked your children what they expect of you? Ever told them what you expect of them? Do you even know what your expectations are? I mean, do clean underclothes really need to be neatly folded in a drawer or just thrown in a drawer until the next time you wear them? An assessment of the way each family member treats the others and of the priorities regarding what is most important of the time-consuming things that we do might create a more harmonious household. Until we did this assessment at family meetings, our mornings looked like this:

"Dragging ourselves out of bed at the sound of the alarm, Ed and I start the routine—making lunches, preparing snacks, signing permission papers, preparing breakfast, and starting the wake-up process. Chrysy and Danny spring out of bed. Kellie covers her head and rolls over. Jenny and Tony move slowly and deliberately around, as if in a trance, and Molly is just going along for the ride. Another day has begun. The countdown begins. 'Ten-minute warning,' I yell between grabbing bites of breakfast and piling all the kids and their stuff into the car. Then it starts—no clean shirt, can't find shoes, lost my homework, and at least one fight over who gets the last Eggo. As usual, even after the warning, we all sit in the car waiting for Kellie to arrive. I drive out

of the driveway hoping to see her come running out of the house, but she just comes when she's ready, knowing somehow that we wouldn't leave her." —Betty

It was every man or child for himself. Our life was filled with reactions to everything. We did not have cooperation. We never had enough time, and we did not know our priorities. Who would have guessed that a few short months after taking parenting classes and starting to use the Belonging Chart, the kids would be knocking on our door to give us a ten-minute warning to take them to school! It did not happen overnight; it required taking one step at a time.

"It is important to realize that the Belonging Chart is a moving target. Once you start playing, you'll realize that your awareness sometimes shifts your own reactions. Something that may have gotten you angry at one time might make you feel surprised or a little inquisitive the next. For example, I became aware of how I set myself up in advance by telling and reminding the kids not to do anything like climbing on the lane ropes when we got into a bank, fast-food restaurant, or airport. Of course, when the whole thing tumbled down and fell on other people, I was furious and upset with the kids. After realizing that I was reacting with this type of anger and knowing that it was just a way for them to get my attention, I started to look at it as a game, and I wasn't angry anymore. It was more like I was on the outside looking in and being inquisitive to see exactly what they were going to do. After I stopped being angry, they just stopped doing it. It was amazing; it's like that whole issue just disappeared, even though previously it was such a big thing. Anyway, that's how it works. As you deal with your own attitudes and change your reactions, the children will have to discover different ways to get your attention. Your goal is to channel them to positive ways instead of negative." —Ed

Why is it that filling the belonging tank is different for each child? One child's tank seems to drain no matter what, and some you just wink at to meet their needs. The difficulty here is that it is the child's perception that determines how much difference the parent's attention will make. We could spend a lot of time with Kellie, but until she knew that she was in charge, her tank would drain very quickly. We had to allow her to be in full control and demonstrate that we knew we could not make her do anything that she didn't want to do. Just showing that we understood her was then enough to fill her belonging tank. It is so much fun to see the game as thinking of every way that you can to build the self-esteem of each child. Sometimes it is a little frustrating when it does not seem to be working as fast as you would like. Fortunately, there are many times when it seems simple to keep the tanks full. For Danny, just going to his sporting events was practically enough. For Chrysy, it was knowing that we would be there when she needed us. For Jenny, it was demonstrating our trust by putting her in charge because she was so capable. Tony was the master of pushing our hot buttons to get our attention because attending his sporting events was not enough. We had to be consistent in noticing and praising him whether we thought he needed it or not. With Molly, all we had to do was wink at her, cuddle her, say her night prayers, and she seemed to be on her merry way. Of course, she was the youngest and got attention from everybody.

The bottom line is figuring out how to focus specialness on each child. As much as possible, demonstrate love, connection, and belonging. There are so many ways to do this, including assisting with homework, reading books, night prayers, playing games, special date night with each child, and attending sporting events and performances and even practices. Constantly find reasons for affirmations, gratitude, acknowledgment, and praise. Let them carry and pass tools while you are working around the house. Give them a paintbrush and let them get messy, especially when outside painting a fence. (As long as they are old enough to know to not eat the paint, it works!) All can help fill the tank. It's fun and real life.

With a little creativity and effort, you can turn almost any negative situation into a positive, affirming one. Instead of saying things like, "No, you can't play with a knife; you might cut yourself," you have to be creative and say, "Oh, it's great that you want to use that knife to see how it works. It is very sharp and can cut many things including your finger. It might work better for you to practice with this spoon right now."

They Are More Important Than Anything Else

Your child must know that she or he is more important to you than anything else in the world. Now, that's a huge expectation. Yes, and you'd better be up for it. Some people will say "Oh, she or he is so needy." Yes, we all are. Some people think you're immature if you want attention. Yes, we all do. We all want these things, but some demonstrate the need more openly than others do. Some children will use positive behaviors to fill the need, and some, as a result of a lack of understanding from the parents, will use negative behaviors. But each child is unique, and don't forget it!

"Why is it the biggest challenge and greatest reward to build self-esteem? It's the biggest challenge because the parent has to take the time and energy out of his or her own busy life of work and caring for the home, etc. to give each child the required sense of belonging. This means designing chore charts so that kids are able to accomplish chores and feel needed by the family. This means taking time and giving opportunities to each child to come up with ideas for carrying out solutions for situations that come up from time to time, like painting the house or shopping for dinner for the week. This satisfies two requirements for self-esteem—being listened to and being taken seriously. It's such a great reward when the resulting high self-esteem gives us fun, joy-filled, exuberant times as a family." —Betty

Families need to spend meaningful time together. This does not mean just being in the same vicinity; rather, it means doing simple things like cooking the family meal, cleaning the house, or washing the car together. Working side-by-side can be a time when children feel relaxed and free to express themselves, and be listened to without interruption.

Doing things together without connecting can actually diminish the sense of belonging in the child. Time spent just sitting and watching TV or a movie without connecting could actually undermine self-esteem and belonging. In addition, if the message on the TV contradicts your family values, it can lead to misunderstanding, conflict of feelings, and confusion. It is important to take advantage and use these as teachable moments in which you connect to what your child is feeling and thinking, and emphasize values that are important for your family. It's not just a cliché; it truly is the quality of time you spend and not just the quantity that makes a difference. Quite simply, you must make time for your family; it needs you now.

Children of all ages need some time when they can have their parents' undivided attention. For busy people, it could mean scheduling family time into your calendar. It also means scheduling time for each child individually and sticking to it.

"Date nights are the bomb. They should happen about once a month and just be fun with no strings attached. They are so important to each child, because that two-on-one time is unbelievable to the child who wants your undivided attention so badly. The child feels special, unique, and truly cherished. We wanted date nights to be a time of special communication, and we filled them with affirmation about school, the way he or she cooperates, and other qualities that we saw in the child. The memories from these events are truly ingrained forever in all of our minds." —Betty

In summary, for the child, belonging to the parent and family is like eating and being satisfied. When the child is full, then there is no more craving until hunger comes again. Each child gets that satisfaction in different ways. Praise, thanks, and forgiveness are three possible ways. Being listened to, feeling needed, and being taken seriously are three other ways. Throw lots of affection and touching in, and you have the formula for huge amounts of satisfaction and tons of belonging. To have this formula is like holding the key to life. "Let's have fun with it," a line from *The Three Amigos*, is truly the way to approach parenting and the game of the Belonging Chart.

Chapter 9
The Importance of Belonging

Passionate Points

We parents are the prize and the goal of each child is to know they belong to us. They get that need met when we pay attention to them. Unfortunately it does not matter whether we are responding to their positive or negative behavior, it only matters that we respond.

Use the Belonging Chart to make parenting a game. Have fun seeing how full your child's belonging tank is and creatively find ways that you can help the child keep it full.

To proactively meet a child's need to belong spend quality time to listen, look into the eyes, ask for side by side assistance, play together, have lots of touching and cuddling and give one-on-one attention to him or her.

Dialogue Questions

What do I like best about the Belonging Chart? How does my answer make me feel?

What are the hot buttons that irritate me the most when pushed by our children? How do I feel sharing this with you?

Family Meeting Sharing Questions

What change am I willing to make for our family to be happier?

What are my favorite things to do on my date with my parents?

Chapter 10

Roots and Wings

There are two lasting bequests that we can hope to give our children. One of these is roots; the other, wings.

—William Hodding Carter, Jr.

What do roots and wings mean to you? Roots and wings, which have been written about and used in songs and poems, are at the core of our dream for a family. Roots give our children a secure stable base, and wings allow our children the freedom to branch out on their own; it is the best model we can offer from our lifetime of parenting experiences. This gives our children a sense of being grounded as they take off to experience the world and all of its ups and downs, goods and bads. No matter how far they go or where they land, they remain connected to the family for love and support, and they bring their unique experiences to nurture and strengthen the rest of the family.

"I have had the experience of walking down the aisle with a daughter on her wedding day. It meant witnessing the focus change when that sparkle in her eye, which had been exclusively reserved for me, went to someone she so deeply and desperately wanted me to love, too. It meant seeing the comfort, reassurance, and joy on her face when I took her hand to lovingly entrust it and her well-being to someone else for the first time. I will cherish those moments in my heart because they are also my reassurance that I have established strong roots and wings and that I'm being rewarded for my efforts." —Ed

Parents want their children to develop into well-adjusted adults who strive to do their best in whatever they choose. This doesn't just happen overnight. It takes years of patient mentoring, consistent guidelines, rules, and above all, an abundance of love that is tangible to the child, even during the most tumultuous times of their teenage years. Many people equate loving their children too much with spoiling them. Love that is most beneficial to children accepts them for the unique individuals that they are. To be a truly loving parent, we need to learn the art of unbiased love. This helps you to focus on the child as a person, rather than on what they do, how they please you, or even the fact that they belong to you. You then learn to accept the possibilities, understand the limitations, and marvel at the individual potential of each of your children. If there are no preconceived expectations, there is less pressure on the child and fewer occasions of disappointment for the parent. When children sense that they are not being measured against their siblings or friends, their confidence grows. There are less disciplinary issues, and above all, they feel valued for themselves.

"I believe that I feel successful as a parent because I'm pleased, content, and happy about who our kids are. I enjoy being with each one and hanging out, continuing to give love and affection. I feel fulfilled, wanted, and needed because they still come to me for nurturing and support. I love that I will always be their mother. I want to be with them in a way that makes each child feel peaceful, happy, challenged, stimulated, and enthusiastic about his or her life." —Betty

It is critical to know what success means to you in your parenting. For us, it is creating a thinking, alive, supportive environment where life can happen. We would feel successful knowing that our kids knew how to love and be compassionate, how to learn and make decisions, and how to be aware of what makes them happy. But to do that, we have to have our own loving and learning skills in order so that we know what makes us happy. The epitome of seeing the results in our life occurred when we went from a battlefield and tug-of-war trying to get the kids to school in the morning, to the place where we would be lying in bed and they would pound on the door to give us a ten-minute warning to be ready to take them to school. This required lots of learning and change on our part. The kids had to see, know, and believe that the changes were real, and we did, too. We had to stop ordering and start asking, stop yelling and be levelheaded, stop getting angry and work out consequences in advance. It is so important to realize that to effect a change in a child, we as parents, or I as a parent, have to change first!

And just when you've spent your life getting it right, there comes the moment when you have to let go because each child should and must lead his or her own life. It is just like the coach on the football field when he realizes that he cannot go onto the field and play the game or, even more ridiculous, play every position. Each child will miraculously choose his or her own path and experiment with life in his or her own way. You can give all the input you want, but you cannot live their lives for them.

The Correct Order

How do you put God first, family second, and self third? This adage has been a mainstay and driving force for us. It is such a call to have priorities straight and feel happy, content, and fulfilled about everything we do. Our family prayer is, "Lord, may others be drawn to you by the way that they see us living and loving in our family." Many of the accomplishments that we have experienced have been unbelievable. To us, though, none of them mean anything without the love and support of each other. Just knowing that we stand strong together as a family makes each recognition or reward much more important to us. The accomplishments in business pale in comparison to the bond of our family. What a tremendous joy to accept an award and look out into the audience to see the entire family sitting together sharing in a job well done. The fact that nearly the entire family is involved in our business together is a tremendous joy.

Because we work and play together as a family, we have the opportunity to experience and share many joyous occasions and special events. It is one thing to enjoy a spectacular sunset by yourself and then fall short while trying to explain it to another. It is totally different to experience the sunset together and then share its meaning and beauty with each other. Setting our priorities is how we made this real in our lives. When it gets difficult to choose, keep this in mind for setting priorities. First, God must be the center of all decisions. This means that we pray as individuals, as a couple, and as a family before making decisions that will impact our lives. While it may sound cliché, "What Would Jesus Do?" is the modus operandi. It gives great perspective when deciding how to handle especially difficult situations.

Next, will it benefit the family? For instance, while it might sound good for you to take a self-improvement course, you still need to ask if you will be able to give enough time and attention to the family now, and will this experience enable you to give more time and attention in the future? And finally, is what you choose to do in life really beneficial to you for now and for the long haul? You may have to make some sacrifices right now that might not feel too good in order to give greater benefit for the near and distant future. It's important to do things for yourself, and I think we often slip into believing that it is selfish to do so. However, it goes back to the truth that you can't give what you don't have. So remember to first keep your own tank full, in a way that has the support of your family.

Our mission is to have a passionate love affair with God, spouse, family, and in our business in a way that attracts others to want what we have and lets them know that they can have it, too. We feel so humbled and blessed and loved and cherished when we think about this.

We never stop being the parents. Even when we're tucked away in a nursing home, sipping our lunch through a straw, we'll still think about our kids and wonder what they're doing. One of the difficult decisions for most parents is whether or not to shield their young children from the harsh facts of life. Sex, drugs, and violence are constantly in the news, and there is no guarantee that life will always be smooth sailing. We have always been careful to choose what the children see on the TV and in the movies. We would filter what they were exposed to based on age and maturity level. When they did observe one of these harsh realities, we would mentor and guide them. If children are taught to face such situations with equanimity, they will be more resilient when, as adults, they have their own challenges to face. It is far better to face these opportunities head on with your children during teachable moments than to fight with or try to rescue them after it is too late.

"What is the wisdom of putting God in the lead and letting go? It is so important to understand that having God in the lead does not mean just allowing things to happen to you and believing that it is from God. We trust that God will give us whatever we ask for, but the biggest problem for most of us is being totally clear about what we want. Then we need to make sure that it is aligned with God's will for good in our world. As long as love is at the center of our intention, everything we dream of comes true. We have created a life in which we can be together with our family and friends, some daily and others whenever we want. We have allowed our priorities to become a reality by following the motto 'dream, pray, and go.' We dream a vision for clarity, tell God what it is and ask for His help, then let go and be open to the people, places, and things that He sends us to help us achieve our dreams."
—Ed

Is It a Value or Just an Ideal?

Our core values are the deeply rooted system of beliefs that govern virtually everything we do in our lives, including education, habits, health, diet, and spirituality. We initially inherited most of them from our parents and our upbringing. So we do it this way because that's what we were told. Sometimes we choose opposite values because we never want our kids to experience what happened to us. The important thing is that once we really get conscious about our values, we can decide whether or not they are serving us. We can also add and exchange values as we go through life. How often have you experienced or witnessed something, nudged your spouse in the ribs, and said, "We should do that"? Whatever "that" is at that moment is an ideal. When you and your spouse actually incorporate it into your everyday life, then it becomes a value.

As we have grown as parents and world citizens, our core values have changed. We hear or read something appealing, attend seminars, observe people whose lifestyle we admire, and when something really inspires us, we strive to make it real in our lives. If it works and we like the results, then we adopt it and add it to our core values. Other things are still ideals that we reserve the right to adopt when our life may accommodate it.

The same core values do not work for everyone, and if you are growing, they will also change with you. We hope our kids don't just blindly take or reject our values. Because they experienced our core beliefs while living in our home, they will have to at least give our values consideration when forming their own.

"Those core values that we believe in so strongly are always inside our children. Most of them were 'caught' and not necessarily 'taught.' When Thomas and Chrysy got their three children baptized at five, three, and one, we knew this truth. Tony knows that the rest of us can't live for long without experiencing his warmth, love, humor, and wit firsthand, so he regularly crosses the ocean back home to Hawaii for a few months to rub shoulders with all of us, but especially his nieces and nephews. This also gives him a chance to savor the nurturing of our home as a refuge. Jenny and Paul encourage their children to do their best in school and to excel and enjoy as many extracurricular activities as possible. Kellie freely gives her healing of Body Stress Release to improve the pain-free quality of life for so many. Molly and Cisco can't just sit around on weekends, but have to explore the natural beauty around their home in Arizona. Danny desires to do the very best for our clients so that they'll have a comfortable and adventurous retirement. When we see the wonderful choices that our children are making, then we know they caught our values." —Betty

They All Grow Up

One minute, there's an adorable, helpless bundle in your arms. Then 18 years go by in a flash, and the next thing you know, it's graduation. Letting go is the final frontier for parents who've made child rearing a major focus of their adult lives. Some parents hang on, propelled by love (of course) and insecurity about how the world will treat their children. Parents who can't let go risk crippling their children's fledgling sense of self-sufficiency. They don't allow their children to deal with the consequences of their decisions. Many parents say that letting go is hard because the stakes seem so much higher today than when they were starting out on their own. Young adults must learn to make decisions for themselves and deal with the results of their choices. Parents can help or hinder that process.

At every stage of their child's development, parents have felt the pressure of making the right choices—whether it's getting their kids into a good preschool, summer camp, or college. Suddenly the major part of their parenting career is accomplished.

Friend, mentor, counselor, refuge, and parent—these and others are the titles we now maintain. Today, half of our children and two of their spouses work with us in our business. We see, interact, and communicate with them virtually every day. On weekends, we cheer at their sporting events and share in the potlucks, go golfing or to the beach, and attend church together. They are our best friends. We truly think that our willingness to let go and support when asked, while avoiding giving advice as much as possible, has helped encourage this relationship. Even when "we have been there before," we resist trying to interfere and allow them to have their own experiences and life lessons. For us, we believe this works for all of us because we started developing this attitude while the kids were still living with us.

Letting go means a period of adjustment for both parent and child. This is most significant when they go away to college or leave home for the first time, but it should be an ongoing process from their earliest years. By encouraging your children's independence, you will help them lead happy and productive adult lives. However, to get to that place of mutual trust and respect, parents must let go. Why is letting go so difficult? We keep asking "Have we done enough?" "Have we given enough?" and "Did they get enough?"

"Tony was the first to leave the nest when he went to college in California. I can vividly remember seeing him off at the airport, and it still brings tears to my eyes. It wasn't worry or concern that he wouldn't be able to handle being on his own; it was simply sadness about not being around him enough. I knew that I would miss hearing his witty comments and funny jokes and experiencing who he was, his personhood and character." —Betty

We know that there is never a time when we will completely stop being parents, but letting go means that we consciously discern whether we let them learn the lesson on their own or assist with wisdom that we can impart, especially when they request it.

Grandchildren

Grandchildren are one of the special gifts that you may receive as you get older. While raising your own children, it probably seemed that you didn't have as much time or energy to spend with them as you wished. Now you can build a special bond with your grandchild. If you have more than one, you should spend quality time with each, individually, whenever possible. Especially if both parents are working, their children may not get enough attention, and you can be the supplemental source.

How can you approach your relationship with grandchildren as a refreshing redo? After all of the ups and downs of parenting, it is super-great to be able to apply what we know now and watch the grandkids respond. They are like sponges and seem to respond to us so much better than our kids did—probably because we are better at it with all of our parenting experience. You don't have to do lots of parenting. It is quality over quantity. You can try things like praising the good and ignoring the bad, to see that it continues to work.

When we are with our grandchildren, we never forget our role to support their parents. One of the keys is to never compare or make bad what the parents are doing and to never make comments that could undermine the parents, especially in front of the kids. If a parent says to stop, to not eat a snack, or go to bed, do not side with the kids by saying, "It's not so late," or "One more wouldn't hurt." You cannot be the parent, so when taking sides, always side with the parents and support them in what they're doing with their own kids. We've had so many opportunities to praise what we like in their parenting and to quietly pray when we see things we don't like.

It is refreshing to leave the front-line parenting to the parents and be the complement to their parenting. There are two prerequisites to accomplish this. First, you must have the relationship, love, respect, and almost admiration of the parents of the grandchildren. After all, only one of those is your child who has grown up with this parenting style and knows how it worked for you. Second, you have to take advantage of the opportunities when parents are present to demonstrate handling situations with the grandchildren so that all can see. This isn't a staged thing like "Watch this," but you definitely want it to be observed and absorbed.

Eenie Meany Minee Moe

Lifestyle, retirement, and legacy planning all require money that both you and your children or grandchildren could use. How do you balance who gets what, and do you ever have to draw a line in the sand to cut someone off? Money is supposed to be a tool to enhance our relationships and lifestyles. Unfortunately, few of us have unlimited amounts, so all money decisions require prioritization. The issue about our children and money is that even when you set your priorities, you have no way to control theirs. For instance, the kids go to Las Vegas and lose money gambling, so you don't want to give them money to repair a roof on the house. Some parents give the kids money to repair the roof, not realizing that it freed up the resources the kids needed to go gambling. If you are going to give to kids, you should expect accountability and communication about how they will be spending yours and their money. If you are not satisfied with the information you are getting but you still want to give them the money, then you will need to make it an unconditional gift and forget it! And, don't bring it up every time you see them, or you won't be seeing them much.

After making sure that the parents have the resources for a long and enjoyable retirement, some families have set up a type of "family bank." The parents put a certain amount of money aside for family members to "borrow." To get the money, they have to present a "business plan" to the "bank board" (other family members), and show a good purpose for the loan, demonstrate how it will be paid back to the bank, and provide information about the community charity that will be positively impacted by the transaction. The family bank does not need to charge interest, especially if someone is borrowing for a residence, which is not designed to generate income. However, if the reason for borrowing is to generate profit, some percentage should go back to the family bank to increase the resource for future generations.

It Isn't Over

Parenting is a journey, not a destination, and it is not an exact science. Expect change and enjoy the journey. That is just the way it is. The main thing is for you and your children to know that you are getting the results that you want in your life. Create an open-door atmosphere so that your children are able to come to you for advice when they are ready. Neither constructive criticism nor giving advice works without openness.

A tree is the perfect metaphor for roots and wings. If it has only one root, the tree will not stand for long. Selfishness doesn't work. Family: three or more roots will be able to hold up the tree, if they work together. There must be a sense of team. More roots: extended family and friends who challenge and support your values. More roots: a church to provide guidance and spiritual support for all. More roots: A community can accomplish great things like overcoming homelessness, hunger, and abuse. The world can achieve world peace. With strong roots, the wings take the love, support, stability, and security out into the family, church, community, and world to accomplish great feats.

We invite you to add a gift from us to your family by simply repeating frequently, "Lord, may others be drawn to you by the way they see us living and loving in our marriage, family, and life."

Chapter 10
Roots and Wings

Passionate Points

God first, family second and everything else follows. Keeping priorities is the surest way to give ourselves the best opportunity to build a firm foundation for our children for when they are ready to venture out on their own.

It's so difficult to say "okay, that's it, you're on your own," but take solace in the fact that even though they are beautifully independent, they will always be bonded to you and your family.

Grandparenting is much less parenting and much more grand! Enjoy it with all your heart; you deserve it!

Dialogue Questions

What are my dreams for our family after the children are gown and leave the nest? How does my answer make me feel?

How will I know I have been a successful parent? How do I feel sharing this with you?

Family Meeting Sharing Questions

What do I want to be when I grow up? What do I want to be like when I grow up?

What do I like most about our family?

LaVergne, TN USA
24 January 2011
213660LV00002B/18/P